STAY MARRIED ABROAD

Stay Married Abroad

BASIL BOOTHROYD

London

GEORGE ALLEN & UNWIN LTD

RUSKIN HOUSE   MUSEUM STREET

PRINTED IN GREAT BRITAIN
in 11 on 12 point Joanna
BY C. TINLING & CO. LTD.
LIVERPOOL · LONDON · PRESCOT

For My Wife

Who isn't any of the wives in this book.
Or so she thinks. Still, I don't
think I'm any of the husbands, either.

B.B.

CONTENTS

PROLOGUE

'It's all right, come in,' said Mrs A, who looked as charming as ever in several sun hats and lemon culotte trousers with a random motif of *ambre solaire* stains. She kicked a frog-flipper off one foot and hung it on the TV brightness control. 'We try to unpack as soon as we get home, otherwise when we want the suitcases next year they're full of sand and punctured neck-cushions.'

The matrimonial investigator is accustomed to calling at inopportune moments, but an offer to come back later is not advisable, even when the witness's home suggests an explosion in the luggage compartment of a small airliner. Clip-board at the ready, I took what was left of a chair full of espadrilles, duty-free cigarettes, assorted aerosols and old French bread.

'When I say we,' said Mrs A, 'I actually mean me, because some of us get a touch of the Viscontis the minute we set foot on our native shore, don't we, darling? Packingwise, it rules us out.'

Mr A was squatting on the hearthrug with a six-strand stole of movie film round his neck, probing the inside of his projector with a sardine key. He wished me good morning and asked me to mind where I put my feet. They were in danger of ruining a vital sequence. 'My laughing French fishermen bit. I'm cutting them in after where she fell off the jetty and sank.'

'Swam under water,' said Mrs A.

'She was gone ages. I kept turning, though, right until she came up black in the face with a seaweed moustache.'

'He promised to leave that bit on the cutting room floor,' said Mrs A. 'It's all very well for him, when the Wainwrights come round, rolling them in the aisles with stuff about here comes the Monster of the Deep, or what price Mother Neptune. More marriages have crashed on holiday movies – '

'There'd be nothing left if you had your way,' said Mr A, scraping up some spilt splicing cement with a town plan of Perpignan. 'What with "Why didn't you tell me I'd got a bra-stiffener sticking out," and "if I'd known you were filming I'd have moved those

11

bottles." All you want is the bits where you're chatting up some wog skindiver with a chest like a burnt lawn.'

'Any film I take – not that he often lets me – he clips out anything where he's standing sideways. When I got him watching some nuns bathing, and his stomach – '

'My stomach doesn't come into it.'

'It came right into that.'

'I cut it,' said Mr A, 'because you'd got me with a little barber's pole growing out of the top of my head, I could just hear your soundtrack for Rob and Jackie Winslow: "Stand by for the Man from Mars, are you receiving me, over." Hello, this is a good bit. Shot of you from behind, prodding that baby octopus. And you needn't gripe about your hairdo, because all it shows is your – '

'Give me that.'

'Cinema vérité, this is.'

'Now, look – '

Q. Er. If this is perhaps an inopportune moment – ?

A. Not at all. We'll put Antonioni in another room, won't we, darling? You won't get any coherent deposition out of him until he's got the whole thing gummed together and coming out upside down and backwards.

Between them, Mrs A doing the heaviest of the work, they loaded the epic footage on to the dinner wagon. 'Besides,' she said, helping it through into the hallway with a light kick, 'he can swear in comfort out there.'

She unwedged a bathing cap from under the door and shut it, listening a moment. 'See what I mean,' she said.

I

'Whiles night's black agents to their
preys do rouse.'
William Shakespeare

Q. *May the court begin by taking evidence about the impact of travel organizations on the marriage?*

WHAT chiefly drives you mad about modern living (said Mrs A) is the gulf between the publicity and the product, don't you agree? Like you get central heating installed because they say Gracious Living at the Touch of a Button, and the first time you touch the button the thermostat falls out of the wall, and you've got a coal-rush on, panning through the dust in the bunker for enough bits to start an old-fashioned grate fire. With travel agencies this goes in spades, not only with the places they send you to, but with the agencies themselves. After all, most of us realize by now that when we turn up somewhere on the Adriatic where there's supposed to be nothing in sight but three old men mending fishing-nets it's actually going to be a riot of transistors . . . though it's a thing the older woman should warn young wives about: a girl called Fancy Carswell, who was at school with me, cried the whole fortnight on their first unspoilt fishing-net holiday, just because she hadn't braced herself for a season of old Ealing Comedies at the cinema and a team of Wall's men pedalling the sands with hot sausages. That was the trouble with my school, bags of hockey and how to turn sheets sides-to-middle, but nothing about real life. Romantic expectations are frightfully fragile. It's best to be finished abroad, of course, if you don't want to be finished the first time you go, wouldn't you think?

Q. *Ah. You were saying?*

A. *I was saying it's best to be finished abroad, unless you want —*

Q. *But before that?*

I shall have to think. Yes. I was saying, the mature marriage accepts that the first thing it sees at Lucerne is a fleet of buses from Notting-ham. What shakes it is that they actually asked the agency to send them, in armchair luxury, to Como, Garda and Maggiore, and there they all are, not even in the right country, with this bit of paper saying that whatever happens they can't get any money back. It takes time and experience to find that the more the agencies advertise themselves as if they'd got Marco Polo for managing director, the more they can't tell an Italian lake from a Swiss one, or an actual running train from something that was lifted out of the timetable just before de Gaulle came back. I've no objection to their boosting themselves on the hoardings until they make Columbus look as if he lived and died in a cupboard, provided when you actually pop in and ask for a couple of weeks at Nafplion they don't go as white as a sheet and get on the phone for some –

Q. *A couple of weeks at where?*

– male nurses. I beg your pardon? Ah, well, there you are. You took the words out of their mouths, if you don't mind my saying so. That's what broke up Lily and Dusty, and without so much as leaving the country. As with all trials of married life, it's fine if the partnership sees eye to eye. One flesh is all right, but one mind beats in every time. The Millers were on thin ice over this even before they got into the agency, because she'd read about Nafplion in a colour supplement and he hadn't. She'd set her heart on it, the way a wife can – and for reasons that often get wives a reputation for whims, I'm bound to admit. Her best line, to interest Dusty in the place, would have been the twenty-pound air fares concession laid on by the Greek Government; the article made a big selling-point about that; instead, she kept reading out bits where it raved about the showers in this hotel having paper streamers across them saying 'Sterilized', which only made him say that he could chalk 'Sterilized' on the dustbins and it wouldn't mean they actually were: also that this was a pretty goof-ball enticement to hook a girl like Lily, who'd stay in a hotel where you had to wash with the horses provided the lobsters were in cheap supply. Oh, my, yes, a woman learns to be selective with her arguments in these things, yet you still get banner headlines every time one of us sets up as a barrister.

But the main trouble was that Lily was all for taking off under their own steam and just going, because this was one of those blow-by-blow articles that told you everything you wanted to know, from the type of goat they made the cheese from to what you could wear on the beach without being arrested. Dusty took the other view:

that a couple who couldn't get from Horsham to Haywards Heath without coming back three times to the middle of Worthing would be out of their skulls to aim for a pinpoint in the Peloponnese without skilled guidance.

'If we've got to go to wherever it is – ' he said.

'Nafplion,' Lily said. 'Some of the maps call it Navplion, or Nauplia, or even Nauplius. It's where Agamemnon sailed for Troy, it says, sacrificed his daughter, Iphigenia, for a favourable wind, then when he got back to Mycenae he was murdered in his bath by Clytemnestra.'

'What's wrong with – ?'

'And Aegisthus.'

'And they put this paper streamer across it, saying 'Sterilized', you told me.'

'Witty,' she said. 'What's wrong with what?'

'Walton-on-the-Naze.'

'What's right with it?'

'You can get there in an hour and a half from Liverpool Street, that's one thing that's right with it, and not sitting in an Italian goods yard with your luggage gone on to Turin.'

'Nafplion's nowhere near Turin,' said Lily, making the best comeback she could in the prevailing conditions. But she was no fool; she saw that if she didn't want a couple of sun-drenched weeks on the Essex Riviera she'd at least better give in over the skilled guidance.

'If you say so, darling,' she said. 'We'll go through a travel agent. There's the one in Battersea the Clooveys use.'

'You mean that one-man hutch outside the power station? Sweets, tobacco, theatre tickets, anti-stammering lectures and villa parties to Alassio for the under thirties?'

'He's never let the Clooveys down.'

'Just because they've risked him a couple of times and never been lost at sea,' said Dusty. 'It's all right for the Clooveys, they just happen to be travel lucky. It's different with us Millers.'

'Why?' said Lily.

'How do I know why? All I know is, if there's a snowball's chance of us getting stranded at the Gare du Nord, sharing double-booked couchettes with a party of Belgian grannies, you can bet your life we'll do it.'

'OK,' she said.

'We'll go with World Wide Travel or no one.'

'Fine,' said Lily, deeming it no time to mention that it was WWT that had double-booked them last time. 'I've got to be in – '

'The big organizations may sting you a bit – '

'I've got to be in the West End on – '

'But at least they know their onions. Just tell them where you want to be – '

'On Friday,' said Lily, 'to buy a new bean-slicer.'

' – and you're there,' said Dusty.

Which shows you how deep-rooted these old myths can get. 'So if you can spare five minutes at the end of your lunch hour we can go together.'

'What's wrong with the old bean-slicer?' he said.

She knew he didn't expect an answer. It was just his way of acknowledging that she'd given in over the Clooveys' man in Battersea too.

* * *

All the men at the agency counter were on the phone when they got there. 'Garmisch-Partenkirchen,' one of them was saying. 'Where's that, then?' So they moved on to the next one, who looked more experienced, as if he'd at least been to one or two of the leading south coast resorts in his time, and perhaps even as far west as Newquay. Besides he happened to be sited in front of a big WWT slogan board saying Ask the Man Who Really Knows.

'Upset?' he was saying. 'They'll have to be upset, then, won't they? How am I supposed to get their baggage back from the Portuguese customs – send a gunboat? Phoning from where, are they? You'll have to spell that for me, hang on while I get a pencil.' He went through a glass door and that was the last they saw of him. After some minutes a girl passed behind the counter eating a pear, and hung the phone up as she went by.

This was a very testing time for Lily, as you'll realize. She'd got an I-told-you-so the size of that illuminated news strip in Piccadilly Circus, handed to her on a plate. Not too good for Dusty. He'd been trying to whistle a bit, and not done too badly at first, but now his lips were getting dry.

'Where is it we're going?' he said to Lily.

'Nafplion,' said Lily. 'Some of the maps call it – '

'Never mind.'

'It's where Agamemnon – '

'All right, damn it,' said Dusty. 'I mean all right darling. I'll try this next chap, he looks as if he's just finishing.'

This was a very tall, thin man with one of those nose bridges that look as if they're going to break the surface any minute. 'You want to give block reservations a rocket, then,' he was saying into his phone. 'It's not my responsibility if we booked – how many? – forty into a hotel they pulled down two years back. Yes, you do that. And the best of Mediterranean luck.' He hung up, wiping his mouth corners.

'Excuse me,' said Dusty.

'Talk about Fred Karno's army,' said the tall, thin man, and suddenly increased his height by about a foot, probably by standing on a hidden stack of obsolete timetables. He called to someone out of sight round the bend in the counter, 'Was that flight one-seven-three?' – and stretched his neck well up into the short waves to catch the answer, which came as faint as a bird's cry.

'Who for?'

'They wanted a Comet.'

'Colonel Walker?' cried the bird.

'One-seven-three's a Vanguard,' screamed the thin man.

'No Comets for Guernsey, not on a Friday.'

'Palermo, Palermo, not Guernsey! Mr and Mrs Pettit, Miss Pettit and a baby!' His neck veins were standing out like a chunky-knit. 'Can you hear me?'

But the distant battery had given out. The thin man stepped down. You try your best, you can't do more.

'Good afternoon,' said Dusty. 'My wife and I want to go to Greece.'

'Oh, yes?' The phone rang. 'Who? Yes, Fred. Could have done, can't remember offhand. Name like Birkett, was it? Tucker, then. That's right, I'm with you. No, no, they were Gibraltar. Night tourist. Wanted Malta, did they? Sorry about that. Still, it's the sterling area either way, so that's lucky. George Langley's trying to get a party of fifteen school-teachers back from Algiers, should have gone to Dublin . . . Well, that's it, you're only human. I didn't leave my pipe round your way this morning, did I? OK, Fred, thanks all the same.'

He hung up. 'Right, sir,' he said. 'You and your good lady off to Spain, is that it?'

'Greece,' they both said.

'Greece, then.'

'We thought,' said Dusty, 'we'd better let you arrange the whole thing for us.'

'That's what we're here for,' said the man.

'Flight bookings,' said Dusty, 'a hotel we've picked out, bit of sight-seeing, travellers' cheques, insurance . . .'

'Yes, yes,' said the man, sounding like Francis Chichester having port and starboard explained to him by a sea scout. 'Just tell me where you want to go, I'll take over from there.'

'Nafplion,' said Lily.

'Never heard of it,' said the man. It wasn't a flat denial that the place existed, but stand a flat denial right beside it and you'd have been pushed to tell the difference.

'It's where Agamemnon – ' began Lily.

'Shut up,' said Dusty. 'The maps sometimes call it Mycenae.'

'No, they don't,' said Lily. 'And don't tell me to shut up.'

'Just let me handle it, will you? What do the maps call it, then?'

'You're handling it,' she said.

'Now, look,' he said. 'It's your idea to go to this damned place, right?'

'Not from this damned place, though. The Clooveys –'

'Rot the Clooveys.'

A boy with unnaturally long wrists came up to them carrying a plump leatherette folder. Behind thick national health lenses his eyes swam like frightened scallops.

'Your tickets,' he said.

'Get out,' said Dusty. 'I suppose you realize it's now three-fifteen. My meeting with – '

'That's all you think of.'

'What is?'

'That blasted office. If you ever – '

'Lucky for some I do. My meeting with Fluid Power Circuits and Machine Tools was at two-thirty, and I'll tell you this – '

'Let go of my arms.'

' – if the deal folds, you can forget a fortnight at the Iphigenia with your sterilised chamber-pots and favourable winds, because by the end of the month I shall be out on the street, and not so much as a wooden handshake, are you listening?'

'Stop shaking me.'

I try to take the impartial view (said Mrs A). He wasn't really shaking her. Just shaking. And, again, it says something for him that he hadn't abandoned hope even now.

It had certainly cheered up the thin man a good deal. It's tedious work, theirs, and little scenes like this, even three or four times a day, help to make it bearable. When Dusty turned on him and bawled 'Give me a map of Greece!' he was hard pressed to scale his happy smile down to a formal smirk. Even then, he still had a laugh up his sleeve, because he fixed Dusty up and had a yellow form and two carbons all completed before he brought the joke into the open.

'And all this is for two persons, is it, sir?'

The worst over, Dusty was cooling off a bit and prepared to cede a point. He looked round to give Lily a shrug. It was as good as telling her she'd been right about big agencies all along. After all, when a man and wife come in to book a married holiday, and after an hour and a quarter the fool at the counter still doesn't know how many in the party –

'Yes, sir,' said the man. 'That's why I thought I'd better ask.'

She'd gone. That was why. It was ironic, really, because she cashed her Ernie bonds, booked for one only through the man at Battersea, and who should be staying in the same hotel at Nafplion but this stress engineer, waiting for his decree. So she's a Mrs McLoostie now, and no travel problems. Goes all over the world with him, stress engineering. If you can hit a seam like that, of course, it's ideal. Last time Mr A and I were in Greece, for instance –

Q. *Just for the record, Mrs A –* ?

– we met this nice young American couple. It was the only time we've ever been away for three whole weeks, and I'm afraid Mr A couldn't resist a touch of –

Q. *What about Mr Miller?*

– status-rattling. So he told these two – I beg your pardon?

Q. *What became of Mr Miller?*

A. *I left that out on purpose.*

Q. *Mrs A, you appreciate that it's the whole truth we're after?*

A. *And nothing but. That's why I left it out. You wouldn't believe me.*

Q. *Oh, come. Isn't it the business of this court –* ?

Q. *All right, you asked for it. He married the deputy matron of a domestic science college.*

Q. *What's so incredible about that?*

A. *At Walton-on-the-Naze.*

Q. *Ah. I agree the pattern has an unlikely symmetry. I'll just make a note in pencil. You were saying?*

A. *You tell me. It's been so long.*

Q. *Status-rattling?*

Thank you (continued Mrs A), yes. So he told these two that we were to be creatures of the sun for twenty-one days solid, hoping to hear that they'd got to be back in Peoria, Illinois, by the Friday, and the man said to the girl, 'When are we due home, hon?' and she crinkled her golden eye-lids and said, 'What's the date now?' 'June,' he said, rolling an iced coke bottle up and down his stomach by muscle control. And she said in that case they ought to try making it back by about the same time next year. 'We could get the project extended,' she said. 'But I guess by then we'll have seen all of Greece there is to see.'

'You could do a year round the islands,' said Mr A. I recognized the inflexion, all right. Sardonic-satirical, you could call it. It passed over their heads, though. They said they'd done the islands last year. What they'd probably be putting up for the next project would be Tahiti. Ought to get a few readings round there, they said.

This was a very bad time for Mr A. It was in the days before the exchange control had padlocked all but the deeper pockets, and when you've squeezed your resources to a wizened nut for the holiday of a lifetime it's not good to run into a couple idling round the Hellenes on a Rockefeller Foundation research grant, first class all the way, convertible Thunderbird provided, and nothing to do but stick a glass rod into the beach of your choice and read off the coral content. Well, perhaps that's not quite fair. Every now and again they had to find an American Express to pick up fresh funds, so they had their worries too.

However, I didn't try bringing him round to see this. It's best to let them have their brood out. But he had a black six days until the tanned young coral hunters moved on for another rugged stint round the Argolis coastline. And even then he kept harking back. Why was he the only man in the world with no perks but a Christmas engagement diary from D'Arcy's Optical Gratings? Did I think we could claim a ruined holiday back from the Rockefellers? And so on. You can't help much when they're as low as this, except by resisting any references to old Mrs Maltby's annual day out at Littlehampton, or the starving multitudes of Bengal.

Luckily, on the Tuesday, I think it was, he ran into a Mr Twiss, from Tamworth, who was only there for the inside of a week, on the compensation from a fall on an icy pavement. After that he quite cheered up and enjoyed life, particularly as this Twiss was still having to get around on a rubber-ended stick. It's these little contributory factors that often make all the difference between success and failure with a holiday, don't you find that?

Q. *Your reference to perks, Mrs A, prompts the question whether your visits abroad have at any time been affected, for better, for worse, by the intervention of persons of influence?*

A. *You mean people like Beefy Gallup.*

Q. *I do?*

A. *It sounds a fair likeness, without an actual identikit to go by. They're a type that a marriage learns to avoid, if it wants to keep together.*

Q. *In what way, Mrs A?*

Sometimes (said Mrs A) you can know them for years without getting under the surface and finding out the truth about them. Then in no time at all they change from hearty, fresh-faced men in smooth double-breasted suits, that you've chatted to at a dozen parties and never seen any harm in, to marriage break-up factors with bells on. Those are your Gallups. Quite suddenly, when you're complaining about having to sell your school-of-Stubbs horse painting with a hole in it to help raise the air fares to Le Touquet – not that you're serious, because the fatal thing with priceless heirlooms in oils is to put them on the market and get nothing but an offer for the frame – and this particular Gallup says, 'You're not trying to tell me you ever pay an airline's asking figure? Look, any time you're flying, just give me a tinkle. If I don't get you on for nothing the least I'll do is halve it, OK?' And it turns out he's the leading freight customer of Stringbag Charter, and his friends are their friends, or else. I'm safe in saying, I think, that a wife at a party, getting the Gallup line, forgets the whole thing as soon as the subject changes to the new bus-shelter design, or dream psychology and rapid eye movement: the danger is when it's the husband who has this chat with the Gallup, and on the way home he talks of nothing but the free flight to Ibiza, and this man at the other end Beefy once saved from drowning, who can't wait to move into a tent and give you the run of his nine-room villa. Men go on about woman's intuition, as if it was something to class with unsightly skin blemishes, but half the rush on the divorce courts is because men haven't got any.

Q. *Skin blemishes?*

A. *You can do better than that.*

Q. *Go on, please?*

Mind you, a wife comes up against the cruel deceptions of life a lot more. After she's accepted a few Grand Free Offers of Sparkling Georgian Tableware, and found that all she gets for her eighty-five wrappers and thirty bob is six tin teaspoons that bend in the jam, she learns to take the world's Gallups with a pinch of salt from the tin with the easy-to-use free-pouring spout, that she can never find under the hermetic sealing without splitting three nails down to the quick. Men are the gullible ones. It's the little child in them. Like to believe in magic. Good fairy Gallup waves a wand, suddenly you're in the best seats at Epidaurus watching Katina Paxinou in Andromache and nothing to pay but the hire of two cushions. And an interesting point here is that your average husband doesn't know Katina Paxinou from Baroness Wootton of Abinger. What's more, he thinks Andromache rhymes with moustache, and if you offered him the pick of the shows he'd plump for Brian Rix's latest with Billy Smart's Circus as runner-up. It's the thrill of sitting free in the middle of the paying customers that gives the thing glamour, even if it's the Polish National Theatre in a verse drama about the Battle of Tannenberg. And this, of course, is the Gallup Effect at its deadliest . . . when a husband is so dazzled at the chance of a cut-price VIP train ride by Trans-Siberian Railway, that it's the last a girl hears of the existing arrangements for a dream holiday on the Costa Dorada.

It was something very like this that split up the Spilsbys. Until then, their holidays had consistently fortified the marriage, chiefly because they were a rare and lucky couple who saw absolutely eye-to-eye on what they meant by getting away from it all, which was anywhere Eastern and smelly, with exotic booze, bazaar-haggling, huge helpings of oily food, and up all night gambling behind bead curtains.

Q. *You said they were friends of yours?*

Only over our dead bodies. It's all I can do to mention them, thanks very much. I just see it as my duty to put them forward as an object lesson you might care to make a note of and thus save much needless grief. I don't say Chloe and Walter Spilsby can't have all the needless grief they can get, as far as I'm concerned; but even the Spilsbys of this world have a right to live out their marriage as they see it, without some Gallup coming along and messing it up. It's harder for them, in fact, when it comes to finding a replacement spouse; it was three years before Chloe came across a Brighton croupier who'd won a pools prize and was ready to spend the rest of his life staking it in the bingo dens of Azerbaijan. And heaven knows how long he'd been waiting, for a soulmate who'd tag along and help him.

It makes the whole case-history extremely interesting, really, the Spilsbys being so strong for the flesh-pots, because you'd think they were the last people in the world to chuck up a month in Tunis, all planned and the deposit paid, just because he met a man who'd befriended a German prisoner now starring as Herod at Oberammergau in the Passion Play. It just goes to show, because this Gallup – actually a tea-broker named Leopold Skillet – no sooner announced that this wood-carver and part time Thespian would get them complimentary seats for the show and a free guided tour of Upper Bavaria than Walter was on the phone washing out Tunis and Chloe was down the vicarage trying to borrow a Bible and get a bit of background. They stood over Skillet while he wrote the letter of introduction in his best BAOR German, rang up the best hotel in the place, and they were off.

Walter and Chloe didn't even know the German for Rien ne va plus, so all they could do the day they got there, which was lateish in the evening, was take the letter round to the stage door, or whatever they have for this production, and wave it at Herod when he came out. He was a bit surprised at first, didn't seem to have heard of Skillet, but his native courtesy came through, and before they knew what was happening he'd walked them back a mile and a half to his cottage type residence and shown them their bedrooms. He was very tired himself, apparently, got a matinee the next day, and it's a very exhausting role, Herod, because you don't get a lot of audience sympathy, so he flaked out on his personal bed and left them to it, before they could even start to explain in sign language that they'd got a three-star booking with private bath somewhere out there in the star-spangled Bavarian night.

And it was about this time, naturally, that Chloe filled her lungs and let Walter have it right between the eyes for getting himself Galluped. She should have done it before they left St John's Wood, of course, but it's a mistake we can all make, not liking to prick the bubble of their joy until it's burst of its own accord. However, she made up for lost time, and didn't stop letting him have it until after the hearing. She liked her sleep did Chloe. So did Walter, come to that, but he saw that he wasn't well placed to complain about a home-carpentered bedstead with a half-inch mattress, because if it hadn't been for him they'd never have been trying to doze off on it. Even when dawn came, which seemed about seventy-two hours later, her censure motion was still in full spate, and with several boosts still to come, as it turned out. Rising betimes, if you could call it rising, and making it back to the hotel, they found they'd been posted as bilkers, on the strength of six quick drinks they hadn't paid for, and their baggage hauled away by the police. That meant a day and a half in jail, and bad luck on Walter that the gauleiter took a kindly view and gave them the same cell, so there was hardly need for Chloe to draw breath. Eleven pounds odd, it cost him, phoning the Foreign Office and the German Tourist Information Bureau in Conduit Street, W1. A lesson to us all, is the way I'd put it.

Q. *Indeed. Why didn't he phone Beefy Skillet?*

A. Phone who?

Q. *Leopold Gallup. I mean — ?*

I know who you mean, yes. Naturally, that was his first thought; well, his second: his first was what he'd give to see him with his nose just showing over a cauldron of hot tar. It took him three calls to find out that he'd gone to America for a year. And by the time he was back, Chloe had pushed through the mental cruelty and they'd divided up the furniture.

Q. *And Walter had got over all thoughts of hot tar?*

A. Time, the great healer. But in any case . . .

Q. *Yes, Mrs A?*

I was just thinking, perhaps I can't claim the Oberammergau affair as a truly classic case of the Gallup effect. Your true Gallup lays everything on all right, but it just doesn't work out. As in our own case, with the original Beefy, the boat train and the Channel crossing. We met him at a British Rail sherry party at Euston station, which is the sort of thing Mr A gets involved with in the course of business, whereas other girls' husbands keep taking them to Embassy receptions in Madrid, and we happened to mention —

Q. *Forgive an interruption, but I seem to have this unfinished note on the Oberammergau affair. You say, and I quote, 'Your true Gallup lays everything on all right, but it just doesn't work out.' Isn't this precisely what occurred in the case of Mr and Mrs Spilsby?*

A. Not precisely. This Skillet had made a slight bish in the ground planning.

24

Q. *And that was?*
A. Sent them to the wrong man. Mixed up Herod and Joseph of Arimathea.
Q. *Ah, I see. Yes, Mrs A?*
Very unusual, for a Gallup (said Mrs A). It's a point of pride with them to show off on the organization side. They set all the proper machinery going; but they can't be on the spot a couple of thousand miles off when the spanners are dropped in. Sometimes, I agree, they don't mention until the last minute, when they call round with your cut-price travel documents, that you'll have to get as far as Venice under your own steam because their sphere of influence doesn't switch in till then. But even that isn't the same as the Oberammergau case. In fact I only know one other like it. Pete and Polly Stevens, this was. Her real name was Theodora, but she was born a Kettle —
Q. *I don't quite —*
A. *Capital K.*
Q. *Of course. Yes?*
— so the Polly stuck, even beyond the altar, and that suited her fine. They were going to Salzburg, and Pete's tailor, a slight drear named Carruthers, said that if they wanted to be shown the best time in the place, with Schnitzels to bring tears to the eyes, look up an old musician friend of his who was on viola with the Bethmann Hollweg string ensemble. So they did this, went round to the band room after a positive feast of Mozart, introduced themselves as friends and patrons of Bespoke H. W. Carruthers Tailor, and the viola player went completely white, tore off his tail suit and threw it at their feet. It actually took a minute or two, Polly said, because he had those old-fashioned long underpants with loops for the braces, and all the time he was undressing he piled violent language on the name of Carruthers, blackening it no little. Being shown the best time in the place wasn't mentioned, nor were Schnitzels. It was very embarrassing. I beg your pardon? Yes, well, I was just coming to that. It took a lot of clearing up. The gist of it was that when the Ensemble had been playing in London the year before, Pete's tailor, himself a frustrated viola man, had sat nightly in the Festival Hall, doting himself silly on the professional techniques, so when this chap walked in one day and asked to be measured for a new suit of working clothes it was as near to a divine visitation as H. W. Carruthers was likely to get. All the proud talk about his old musician friend was laying it on a bit, but that happens with hero-worship. The friendship was simply the viola player looking at himself in six

mirrors, and Carruthers scuttling round on his knees with a mouthful of pins. What's more – and this shows how even a bespoke tailor's heart can be touched, when he sent out the bill and it just stayed out, he regarded it as a small price to pay for such a thrilling association, and forgot it. Literally.

Q. *Are you trying to tell me* – ?

A. I'm telling you.

Q. *But what tailor would* – ?

A. Bespoke H. W. Carruthers Tailor.

Q. *Oh, well, if you say so. But my own tailor, an old-established and respected man in the Grays Inn Road, despite a lifelong connection* –

A. Excuse me, but haven't you gone over to the A? You're supposed to be the Q. Or can I ask you a Q?

Q. *By all means.*

A. This is going to look idiotic when your report comes out. My Q is simply do you think I'm making all this up?

Q. *Why should you?*

A. Exactly. And we're back in our corners, I think.

Q. *Will you kindly continue?*

He literally, as I was saying, then, forgot. It was the viola-player who remembered. Night after night, throbbing away there in the tenor clef, it had kept coming back to him that his tails weren't paid for. That's the artist's temperament for you, keenly alive to unfulfilled obligations, but somehow never getting around to fulfilling them. So it was understandable that when his conscience unexpectedly showed up, clothed with the flesh of Polly and Pete Stevens, crying the name Carruthers and obviously sent to collect either the suit or the money, something snapped, and it wasn't a string.

Q. *Thank you, Mrs A. And the incident had a deleterious effect on the Stevens marriage?*

A. Indirectly, yes. Pete went to a new tailor who cut waistcoats straight across the bottom like egg-cosies. Polly, who hadn't noticed until then how his figure was going . . .

Q. *Yes. I hardly think we can* – er. *Could we turn to the matter of the original Beefy, the boat train and the Channel crossing?*

A. If I could go over to a Q again, why don't we keep that for tomorrow? I understand you'll be hearing submissions on general matters of holiday transport, and if that doesn't qualify I don't know what will. Besides, I could do with a drink. What about you?

Q. *A very good Q, Mrs A. And one I could scarcely have asked, of course.*

II

'There's nothing under heav'n so blue
that's fairly worth the travelling to.'
Robert Louis Stevenson

YES, indeed (said Mr A) I can certainly tell you in my own words about Beefy, the boat train and the Channel crossing. I'd just like to say first that any husband who doesn't want to be up all night reading the small print in the Matrimonial Causes Act could do worse than brush up on a better known incident – the one about Queen Elizabeth . . . the first, I mean –

Q. *Hasn't she gone out of service?*
A. In sixteen hundred and three. *What's that got to do with it?*
Q. *I think perhaps I'd better ask the questions. We got into some confusion over this yesterday. I take it you don't allude to ships?*
A. Only British Rail packets, Dover to Calais, jammed to the gunnels on an unusually hot day in August. *Why do you ask?*
Q. *There you go again. Should we make a fresh start?*
A. If you say so. The court strikes me as a bit testy this morning. I hope it slept all right?
Q. *Please. However, since you ask, it did dream about a viola-player called Mrs McLoostie prospecting for coral at Oberammergau, but it intends to preserve its impartiality all the same. What about Mr Gallup, the boat train and the Channel crossing?*

Certainly (resumed Mr A, giving the court a look). If I could just make the point about Queen Elizabeth, Walter Raleigh and the cloak in the puddle. The fact is, there's nothing a woman likes better than a bit of red carpet, as long as it isn't one where the fluff comes off and chokes her Hoover up to the handle grip. History has its blank spots, but I'll bet when Francis Drake came rushing in from Spain to show HM her first potato, it didn't go anything like as big as Walter Raleigh's bit of flannel. All it cost Walter was a couple of groats at the dry-cleaner's, and there was poor old Francis, been twice round the world for this priceless tuber, and nothing from the throne but a sniff, and possibly the comment that it reminded her of Mary Queen of Scots on a bad day. There was more woman in her than we've been led to believe.

I'd known this Gallup for some time as a man on the eight-twenty-three with a different looking ticket, but he might have been an animal foodstuffs tycoon for all I knew. I like to keep train relationships pretty formal, myself, otherwise you haven't read the headlines before they strike up with a full specification of the duck-run they're building, or how their wives got on the wrong side of the window-cleaner. I wouldn't even have known he was called Beefy if someone hadn't wished him goodbye with it one day when he got out at East Croydon. I remember it because I thought they said Fifi, at first, which was a bit startling for fifteen and a half stone and a ginger chin beard.

But there you are, it took Mrs A less than five minutes at a rather sumptuous party for British Rail top brass – all outside catering, none of your sausage rolls that squeak when cut – to find that he was BR's head man on window-catch design, or restoring blacked-out teeth on posters. He was also quick to admire a girl's ear rings, Moorish-type cocktail jacket and nail-varnish shade, so he'd have been outstanding value even if he hadn't said he could make her a VIP at the lift of a telephone.

Personally, I'd have kept quiet about our forthcoming week in the North of France. It was one of our poorer years – and nothing to do with Exchange Control; even if they'd let us take gold bricks we still couldn't have got much farther south than Boulogne. Many of those present, by the look of them, had wintered in Fiji, popped home to revise their investments portfolio, and were off any time now to dear old familiar haunts in the Caribbean; the rest, I expect, would be vacationing on one of those reciprocal arrangements with Continental railways that gets a family of four to Messina and back at parcel rates. I've often wondered, myself, whether Continental railwaymen feel they're getting a fair swap over these concessions, actually. When you think of all our laughing stationmasters steaming south in luxurious punctuality to palm-fronded Antibes and points west . . . and their oppos over here, stuck outside Macclesfield in an old football special with its stuffing hanging out –

Q. *May I just – ?*

A. — and nothing for ash-trays but screw-holes . . . Please do.

Q. It's more on a point of private curiosity, Mr A. Surely on this occasion, surrounded by the privileged in one form or another, you should have welcomed Mr Gallup's offer to smooth your path? Yet your attitude seems somewhat —

A. I'm thinking beyond the offer to the smoothing, which may be causing the occasional sour inflexion. I would ask the court to be patient.

Q. As always. Yes, Mr A?

His offer, in fact, was more labour-saving than actual money in the bank. Just a matter of putting us in the personal charge of his conductor on the Golden Arrow, and when we got to Dover we were on no account to move, dear lady — I'm afraid some of this is reported speech, all right? — because he'd have a man come and get all our gear, whip us through the Customs and straight on board into our cabin, where refreshments and service would be waiting. We had a cabin, of course?

'We've got a cabin, of course?' said Mrs A, dragging him over with both hands, through the cream of railway society.

'Oh, it's you,' we both said.

'I was telling your good lady she mustn't think of roughing it on your French trip.' And he wedged in quickly — 'Or you either, I mean.' Got reserved seats, had we? Ah, pity. Still, that was no problem, always had a few kept back for VIPs.

I didn't like the sound of this. For two reasons. You can be born a VIP, go everywhere between serried ranks of MI5, and know that when you get there, wherever it is, there won't be a twig out of place, and anyone with unsightly trousers will have been shoved behind a fence. Or you can grow into it, provided you can hang on to the top of the charts long enough, like Prime Ministers or David Frost. It takes a bit of getting used to. The first time a man brushes your hat and puts it on for you before you leave home it's quite a shock. 'Don't you worry with that,' you say to him. 'Men are born equal, and that means you're as good as I am.' But of course he's been trained in the VIP world, and he goes on brushing it and putting it all the same, also making sure that when you get to New York or Tananarive, whatever it says on the tickets you haven't even seen, your detective story's open on your bedside table at the page you left it last night, and your tooth-paste, which you have a habit of squeezing in the middle, is straightened out and folded up neatly from the bottom. In a week or two you've stopped complaining about this sort of thing: what you complain about now is when you find you're out in the street without your hat on, because this damned, incompetent idiot wasn't quick enough with it, and put it on the leading aide trooping out behind you. Oh, yes, you can grow into it, all right. What's useless is to be the casual or spasmodic VIP, who spends three hundred and sixty-four days making his own way in the world, and suddenly, on the three hundred and sixty-fifth, he's got a lot of people polishing his fountain-pen, checking his route for smells and helping him on with his pre-warmed underpants. This can only mean a disastrous shock next morning, when he comes down and the sink is blocked, the post full of parking summonses, and not a soul in sight with a decent bodkin to winkle out the end of his pyjama cord that's lost itself round the back of the slot. I'm not labouring this?

Q. *And the other reason?*
A. *You certainly keep track of an argument, I'll say that.*
Q. *Thank you. Go on, please?*

Well, I want to put this kindly. I was sorry to see that Mrs A, a girl of discrimination in so many matters, had swallowed this Gallup like an oyster. It's always distressing to see a loved one deceived, but extremely hazardous to a marriage to suggest that anything of the sort is happening. You and I, I think I can say, don't place too much reliance on promises made at cocktail parties, solemn undertakings to introduce us to Orson Welles, give us a grand piano they can't fit in the new flat, or come round first thing Sunday morning to show us how to siphon out the fish pond and dredge up the light-meter we've dropped in it. In younger, more callow days I'd sit around for weeks, with my hair well brushed and the drink tray at the ready, waiting for Orson or the piano, wasting valuable time I could have spent reading up on pond-siphoning. But nothing happened, of course, and I know now that nothing ever does.

So when your wife comes up with a flush of girlish excitement and another false prospectus, all charm and ginger whiskers, you don't know whether to take her in your arms and whisper the facts of life, or tell her not to be a crazy fool. A wife, what's more, hasn't any resentment over being VIP for a day. She's all for gathering rosebuds, and when they turn back to onion skins next morning she couldn't care less.

'And that's the last you'll hear of that,' I told her, driving home.

'It'll be absolutely fabulous,' she said.

'Fat fraud.'

'Imagine, in the personal charge of the conductor.'

'Personal phoomph,' I said.

'And the most marvellous thing, none of that degrading fight for porters at Dover. And he's laying on a cabin for us, by the way. He was a bit shaken when he found we hadn't got one.'

'You don't listen, do you? Men like Gallup – '

'One thing, though,' she said. 'We shall have to get some new luggage. You can't be VIPs with all your catches bust and a rope round. Besides, we shall be travelling First. You can't be a VIP – '

'Now, look – '

'You'll never make it!' she said, as some lights turned amber.

But there we were, as I'm sorry to say it turned out the following Monday week, sitting in the first class in our new hat, coat and handbag, and we'd hardly got through Penge when a man in a gold headdress came paging us, and if he didn't get the name absolutely right it was as near as made no difference. He had three stewards with him, one each to lift our feet on to little footstools and another with smoked salmon sandwiches, a bottle of nicely chilled hock and if there was anything else we required would it be too much trouble to touch the bell.

'Oh,' she said, looking at the hock.

'Madam?'

'Isn't there any champagne?'

'But of course,' said the man.

I tell you. When they ride on the crest, they ride on the crest. It seemed to me that I could only resign myself. Gallup was paying off, and she hadn't even said she told me so. On the other hand I was getting twinges of conscience. With the railways losing a hundred and forty millions a year, was it right to accept largesse on this scale? At any rate, I told myself, somewhere just past Canterbury, I should insist on giving the stewards ten bob. The man in the gold headdress was obviously well up in the rarefied regions of non-tipping. I was half inclined, in fact, as we rolled smoothly on towards the white cliffs, to insist on paying for the refreshments.

'I think I shall insist,' I told her, 'on paying for the refreshments.'

'You don't think he'll be furious?'

'Who?'

'Gallup.'

31

'I don't care if he is,' I said, fearless with Heidsieck.

'Anyway,' she said, 'I don't suppose they'll let you.'

This, I must say, had occurred to me.

'I trust everything has been satisfactory?' said the man in the gold hat.

'Absolutely fabulous,' she said.

'Very good, indeed,' I said. 'Thank you very much. By the way, I'd like to insist on – '

'Our orders were to look after you to the very best of our ability.'

'You've certainly done that,' I said.

She said they'd been fantastic.

'Thank you very much indeed,' he said. 'So that will be just five pounds ten, including the Pullman supplement.'

'Hey! Just a minute,' said Mrs A.

'We're running in, darling,' I said – 'if you want to pop down the corridor or anything.'

I gave the man six pounds. He put it in his pocket and waited. I gave him another ten bob, he said it had been a pleasure, and moved off to let the three stewards close up and ask if everything had been satisfactory.

'Forty-two pounds odd,' I told Mrs A when she came back. 'I mean, including the new luggage, hat, coat, handbag, Pullman supplement, the difference between third class and – '

'Don't spoil it,' she said. 'You always have to spoil things. Besides, we're just going to sit here now until the man comes, that's going to be fabulous.'

Well, I have to admit it wasn't altogether displeasing to see our unprivileged fellow passengers panicking right and left, jumping off the moving train, pushing their luggage out of the window at each other, grabbing porters by the waistcoat and hanging on to them by main force. And us just sitting there, knowing everything was going to be taken care of.

'Just look at them,' said Mrs A, dreamily. 'They're positively fighting each other.'

'Degrading,' I said. 'Not to say exhausting. Start a holiday like this, you haven't recovered by the time you're due to come back. There's a man along there carrying four suitcases and a hat box, looks as if he'll hardly make it to the Customs.'

'It's heaven,' she said. 'I suppose you can't see our man? I should think the train's about empty now, except for us.'

'Well,' I said, 'there's a very, very old man in a sort of Gay Nineties bowler, coming along looking up at the carriage windows.'

'No, no,' she said. 'That's not him.'

But it was. It was him. The man in the gold hat had gone, the stewards had gone, everyone else had gone, there was just us and him. He wasn't too pleased, as it turned out. Not nasty, but you know what old people are like when they meet you off a train and you're right at the far end of it, with four suitcases and a hat box.

'I'm Mr Bishop,' he said, checking our labels with a note on his Woodbine packet. After a break for wheezing he went on to say that it was his last day on the railways, retiring tomorrow, not giving up work, though, he'd seen too many go that way, weren't we going to get the bags out, then, and did we know Mr Gurney?

'Gallup,' I said. 'Mr Gallup.'

He brushed it aside.

'Very nice gentleman, Mr Gurney. You don't want to give up work, not after your active life, he says. You'd fade away. Fade away, he says. You can start with me any time, he says. Night watchman.' He told us his married daughter's views on this, and slipped in a longish passage about the scandalous rise in council house rents, and why his first wife had left him. I missed some of it, getting out the four bags and the hat-box. Far away beyond the waste of empty platforms, the boat was blasting off its siren.

'Right,' I said. 'Where to now, then?'

'Up the pickle factory,' said Mr Bishop. 'Gurney's pickles.'

'No, no,' I said.

'Won't you need a trolley,' said Mrs A. 'Sort of barrow thing?'

He sucked his breath in like a Westinghouse brake. Daren't touch the baggage, he said. Union trouble, see. Lay a finger on the baggage, they'd go up like a gas main. No one touched the baggage, only porters.

'What about a porter, then?'

He looked at me as if I'd suggested a Heron of the Queen's Flight. All gone, the porters. In the Customs, on the boat. No bloody porters, we wouldn't get. But we weren't to worry. He'd think of something. 'Right, sir. You pick up those two, I'll tuck the two small ones under your arms, and if the lady can manage the hat-box I'll lead the way.'

If he'd been carrying anything we should never have made it. He was no sprinter at best, and telling us the story of his life meant frequent stops for oxygen and coughing. We should probably think he was a liar, he said, but he went right back to the old London, Brighton and South Coast, remembered beer at twopence a pint and Queen Victoria's funeral.

They were surprised to see us at the Customs. Everyone was through and away but us, and the officers were taking their coats off and lighting cigarettes.

'Specials,' said Mr Bishop to one of them. If he hadn't mentioned it I don't think we should have had any trouble. As it was, suspicions were quickly aroused, and the man put his coat on again and asked for the suitcase keys. He was thorough. He had a close look inside Mrs A's wristwatch, held one of my shirts up to the light, broke an aspirin in half and took it into a back room for some minutes. We had the feeling, moving at last to the gangway, that he was already on the RT to the douanes over the water – keep your eyes skinned for a hot, agitated couple with trembling hands, obviously hiding something but I couldn't spot what.

At the bottom of the steps we paused to thank Mr Bishop for all he'd done and say good-bye. He wouldn't hear of the good-bye. More than his job was worth, what was left of it, not to see us properly fixed up on the boat; very, very nice table for two at lunch, couple of window seats afterwards in the first class lounge. If we'd just give him a hand up the gangway . . .

Mrs A had to give him the hand. I hadn't got one. The ship was so full they wouldn't have sailed from Dunkirk. It was no good telling him we didn't want any lunch, all we wanted was for him to get the hell out of there and leave us to fight for our Lebensraum as if we weren't VIPs at all.

'The cabin!' said Mrs A, suddenly remembering. 'We can go to the cabin.'

'Keep close behind,' said Mr Bishop. 'We don't want to get separated, not in this lot. Cabin? Didn't say nothing to me about no cabin.'

Perhaps you've never dragged a wife, four bags and a hat-box round a cross-Channel steamer in August, I don't know. It was lucky we had a spearhead. He went in at the fast butt, even through the queues jamming the doors of the dining saloon. When he was near enough he groped through the press and seized the Chief Steward's sleeve. 'Two very, very nice seats for lunch,' he said. 'Friends of the general management.'

'Don't be a silly old bleeder,' said the Chief Steward, plucking himself free to rap out seamanlike orders on cruet dispositions.

In the end Mr Bishop left us wedged against the funnel, over the rich fumes of an engine room hatch and shuddering to the vibrations of the siren.

'I'll be going then, sir,' he said, but not in fact going, even though the first gangway chains were being rattled free. When he'd got his pound he made a fair turn of speed, though, and we always assume he got off all right. Does the name Apsley Cherry-Garrard mean anything to you?

Q. *I'm sorry, you caught me off guard for a moment. Apsley* — ?

A. *It's just that he went to the South Pole and wrote a book called 'The Worst Journey in the World'. Mrs A and I think this proves he wasn't on that boat.*

Q. *Indeed, yes. You didn't, I trust, adopt any attitude of I-told-you-so towards Mrs A in this matter?*

A. *I thought about it. Husbands are only human. But if these things aren't said at the time, they qualify as raking up the ashes of the dead past, widely recognised as divorce material. On the other hand, no husband worth the name, with his wife wedged on one leg against a hot funnel, crying over her holed nylons and trying to think of the French for heel-bar . . .*

Q. *Professional wrestling?*

A. *Ladies' shoe repairs. But, in any case things went so well at Calais, it seemed best to try and forget, with a tiny footnote to keep clear of all Gallups, wherever they may be found.*

Q. *Went well in what way?*

A. *We were clear of VIP territory by then, that's in what way. Hardly got a line ashore when smiling French porters grabbed the bags. On the train in five minutes flat with two very, very nice seats for lunch.*

If you've ever taken the Southern Region from Littlehampton to Portsmouth (said Mr A) via Fishbourne Halt, Bosham, Nutbourne Halt, Emsworth, Warblington —

Q. *Shouldn't we perhaps* — ?

— Warblington, as I was saying, Halt, Fratton, Havant, Bedhampton Halt, Hilsea Halt — Yes?

Q. *I feel bound to point out that my terms of reference are foreign travel only.*

Wait for it (said Mr A). Anyone who ever did that trip might think themselves pretty well schooled for another one on similar lines, namely from Genoa to Finale. The distance is about the same, also the sense that all the stations have practically adjoining platforms. There are differences, of course. It's hotter in Italy, the journey takes four hours instead of one and three-quarters, and at least the English loudspeakers speak English, even if you can't get hold of anything much but the announcer's s's; not panicking away in a lot of excitable Italian that could be telling you the train's on fire. It takes longer, not only because there are more stations to the mile, so the driver daren't get rolling in case he runs past them, but because he climbs down each time to chat up buddies, take wine or pat goats, and at least once, the time Mrs A and I were aboard, backed up again into the last stop to finish a talk he'd been having with the station-master's dog. I'm sorry? No, well, I admit I wouldn't swear to it. Just the impression we got. We weren't observing too keenly by then, because we'd been travelling all night and lost the luggage in Genoa.

'Not the luggage, the tickets,' said Mrs A, coming in with a jug of orange juice, floury arms and three glasses. 'I thought I'd better just check that he wasn't perjuring himself, and what do I find?'

'That's not just plain orange juice?' said Mr A.

'Right.'

'Pour me one.'

'Have some orange juice, not plain,' said Mrs A.

Q. *That's extremely kind. May I?*

'I agree this was the holiday when the tickets didn't turn up,' said Mr A. 'We went through a little man at Battersea, recommended by those fools the Millers.'

'By the Clooveys.'

'Split hairs,' said Mr A. 'By the Clooveys to the Millers.'

'But they didn't *go* to him, darling, they just recommended him to us. They went to World Wide Travel and practically had their separation in the vestibule. I've deponed on all this. As a matter of fact, we didn't go to him either.'

'We did.'

'No,' said Mrs A. 'We went to WWT. Don't you remember those fat envelopes flopping on the mat the whole week before we were due for the off, all printed "WWT for the holiday where Nothing can go wrong," with the nothing in purple underlined in green, and every time we thought it was the tickets it was enormous brochures for Morocco, Corfu, Bilbao, six weeks in China from eight hundred guineas and gay Magyar nights in the Hungarian goulash country?'

'I don't think it would be right to waste the court's time in a matter where it's only one witness's word against another,' said Mr A. 'The point I'm making is that we had to miss the boat train and hire a car to Southampton so that we could spend the morning in the agency while they made out what they kept calling duplicates and treated us like zombies for losing the ones they'd never sent, right?'

'Not when I came in.'

'What?'

'The point you were making when I came in,' said Mrs A, 'was that we'd lost the luggage in Genoa, which isn't the same thing.'

'It was the same holiday,' said Mr A. 'I went into the Ladies on Genoa station while the porter – '

'Two little words,' said Mrs A. 'Signori, signore, and he can't tell them apart.'

Q. I'm still not completely clear, Mr A, on the precise point you are making?

A. I'm only just making it. That's how she came to take up flying.

Q. Oh, yes. Yes. I suppose you wouldn't care to be a littl more specific on that?

At one time (said Mr A) my wife was a dedicated train-lover. She'd probably deny this, if she wasn't back in the kitchen, swelling the dish-washing backlog with some hundred-ingredient recipe she's ripped out of a magazine in the hairdresser's, but that would simply be as a matter of principle and I know you'd have the good sense to set her testimony aside. During this time –

Q. You didn't think she came rather well out of the recent clash on the luggage, the tickets, Cosmic Travel and the Clooveys' man at Battersea?

A. You were asking me about the way she took up flying.

Q. I'm sorry. Yes?

During this time (continued Mr A) she had what was more or less a set speech about the crazy modern lust for speed, and the way a jet to Nice in an hour and a half couldn't compare for sheer enjoyment with the long, leisurely rail journey across France, the thrill of waking to the clash of midnight buffers, peeking through the window-blind at the romantic bustle of Dijon station by moonlight . . . then dawn's pearly fingers, the first palm trees, a splitting headache, nowhere to shave and cramp in all limbs – well, she never mentioned that, actually. But that was roughly how she carried on, especially in the last week or two before the off, when the TV newscasts release all those items they've been saving up for this time, about planes with jammed flaps circling Gatwick, or coming in at Orly with an engine alight, or taking off at Ringway through a raft of power cables. You know? Or just plain flying into an Alp.

Oh, yes. She only had to see headlines saying 'Gunman Runs Amok in Caravelle', and she'd be raving about the waiter service on the Swiss railways. And as for the old films they always show just before we pack, the ones with the flight crew in a food-poisoning coma, and this Boeing being talked down in the fog with a passenger at the controls who doesn't know his altimeter from a Westminster chiming clock, they'd send her dead lyrical. Any railway PRO who heard the way she went on after one of those films, about the romance, luxury and dependability of the iron horse, would have been in there baldheaded, with a handsome offer to travel around the system shrieking her stuff from the backs of guards' vans.

But the missing documents, lost luggage and four hours' nervous collapse by rail marked a turning point. First hints were when I began to find airline literature strewn casually around the house where I couldn't miss it. She'd wanted, she said, to look up the spelling of Düsenflugzeugen for her German evening classes; or pretended that Caroline Barratt, who'd flown everywhere for years and been cut to ribbons many a time for being a blind little fool, had told her it was the only place to find a special three-way-stretch girdle ad. They're devious, but smart. Next year, when she suddenly murmured, 'Why don't we fly?' I realized I'd been primed for months.

Q. *And you were naturally delighted?*

A. *Speaking as a man who managed nearly four years in the air force before they found he'd never left the ground, no.*

Q. *But Mrs A took to it like a, shall we say, bird?*

A. *And we shall say it again. Her trouble is, she's never been caught over Biggin Hill with her nose wheel dropped off – because they got me in the end,* even with faulty colour vision and suspected varicose. She's done too many uneventful flying hours, that's the difficulty.

Q. And never looked back?

A. I'm the one who looks back – for any hairline cracks in the tail assembly. Or, in the case of air ferries, to see if the cars have worked loose, all set to burst through into the passenger compartment the minute we dip for the glide.

Q. Thank you. The question of the marriage, the holiday and the motor-car is one, incidentally, that I have a note to examine. Would you be prepared to testify on that?

A. Certainly. If it's complete impartiality you're after I'm the obvious witness. I don't say that Mrs A would lie deliberately –

'Lie about what?' said Mrs A, framed attractively at the window in a riot of floribunda.

'I was saying,' said Mr A, 'that some wives would lie deliberately on the only beach bed and leave their husbands to the big sharp stones. Whereas you, my heart's flower – '

'I've told him before,' said Mrs A. 'When he's lying his nostrils go pink. If anybody wants a beer and some slightly failed bouchées aux champignons I got from a magazine at the hairdresser's, they're out here in the garden, all right?'

The court rose.

III

'What wilt thou do to entertain
this starry stranger?'
Richard Crashaw

―――――――

I HOPE this report's going to end up with a few useful tips (said
Mrs A). Your last one*, apart from warning girls to avoid husbands
who use tray-purses, and men not to sulk when they find that their
wives run knock-knee'd, rather left the matrimonial public to draw
their own conclusions. So a hint you might like to jot down –

Q. *I came out strongly against flute-lessons as training for motherhood, I
fancy? Also recommended husbands not to laugh off a wife's tendency to smell
mice?*

All right, if you think that puts you up in the Stopes, Spock and
Cartland bracket. I was only going to say that a maxim for wives,
and they need all they can get, is to let a husband have his romance
out, and not keep unmasking his swans as geese, a sure way to lose
him to the first woman's magazine writer he runs up against. This
is just what happened to Minnie Thatch, in fact, on a luxury coach-
tour of classical Greece. They were somewhere near Thebes, and Don
Thatch had had his eye out of the window for about forty miles,
looking for the crossroads where Oedipus killed his father. Then
just as they got there, luckily slowing up behind a bunch of rush-
hour Thebans commuting by donkey, Minnie grabbed his arm,
pointed ahead and said, 'Goodness, look at all that gorgeous manure.'
It's true the stuff had been frightfully short in Willesden, but of
course nothing was further from Don's mind than rhubarb just then.
In any case, as he said to us afterwards, what chance had they got of
getting it through the Customs? I thought it was a brave try at a
joke, and fell about accordingly, but Mr A told me later that when the
Thatches had rented a cottage in the Cotswolds one year Minnie had

* *Let's Stay Married.*

made Don bring up the compost heap in a plastic bag every Monday for their garden in London.

This wasn't the first time that trip she'd snatched at his rose-coloured glasses and nearly torn his ears off. They'd been to Olympia the day before – What? I'll bet that's what she'd do, make some crack about Earls Court. I'm sorry, I realize you have to get your facts right – and although Don could take javelin-throwing or leave it, and wasn't at all hooked on the thrill of athletes' damp singlets – which I often think Colonel Teddie Tinling could turn his mind to one of these days when he's finished the year's Wimbledon knickers – Well, if you've ever been to Olympia you'll know that spiked shoes and starting pistols don't have to enter your thinking. What enters it, if you've got the sensitivity of an armadillo, is intoxicating draughts of old world peace, annihilating all things made to a green what-is-it, never mind. This got Don like a beakerful of the blushful Hippocrene, and he was drinking deep, with his eyes closed and the scent of sweet grasses swirling in his pipe smoke, when Minnie comes trotting out from behind a temple, towing an American with a macintosh cover over his hat. 'Darling,' she yells, 'you simply must meet Mr Weitzeimer, he makes nose-cone metal for ballistic missiles.' So what with that and the Oedipus complex, and the bad show at Salamis in between –

Q. *What happened there?*
A. *Sort of Greek Trafalgar, where they sank the Persians.*
Q. *Thank you. But in connection with Mr and Mrs Thatch?*

I think it was Minnie's worst, myself. Don was gazing out over the straits, seeing it all so clearly in his mind's eye that he naturally wanted her to share the fun. But when he tried to tell her, she kept shushing him until she'd finished a debate with a Mrs Purvis, from Ilfracombe, on the rival merits of brand-name gravy-thickeners. So they'd hardly got home from that holiday before he fell in with Storm Tarragon, real name Bertha Fittle, who wrote long completes in *Woman's Wiles* about clean-cut young geologists and girls from Girton, quoting Keats to each other and living it up in the Aztec country. I don't know how he came to read the stuff, but they do say a man seldom misses the chance to skim through the ladies' weeklies. If you catch him at it he pretends he's checking on what he gets for the month's paper bill. Anyway, they were married inside the year, and it couldn't have turned out worse. He found she kept romance for the printed page. In private life she spent all her time running rate-payers' action groups, making speeches in her sleep about bus-shelter design and projected drainage schemes. Saddest case I know, really, even counting the Dawson-Weekses and the Majorca stalac-tites, which –

Q. *Mrs A, as time is running a little short – ?*

A. *I'm as anxious to get on as you are. Does the court realize how nearly Mr A's finished his movie editing? Once that's on its launching pad we've had it. He won't even wait for the hours of darkness and the full-size picture, which I used to think I could rely on at one time. He'll run it small-screen on the back of an envelope, with a tiny little tousled me, all bright green sun-tan and no teeth because he's foozled the light meter, all right?*

Q. *Indeed. Will you be good enough to proceed?*

I wouldn't quite put Mr A in the Don Thatch bracket. He can't take much of the classical drama in a Roman amphitheatre, for instance, before he starts the commentary on which bits of him have gone numb on the marble. But he's a lot in common with Gerald Queenbridge and the seed-packet effect, more of which in due course. We call it the UPS or Underpants Syndrome in his case, and it's a matter of getting uncontainably furious with anyone who isn't responding properly to atmospheric overtones. The original underpants belonged to an Air Commodore he used to tag about with just after the war in the capacity of right-hand man and cringer, with airline tickets to romantic places – also cigarettes that bore a lipstick's traces, I shouldn't be surprised, not that it was any of my business at the time. And all at the tax-payer's expense. The UPS struck beside the Dead Sea, after an inspection tour of RAF blanket, boots, webbing and cap-badge dumps. For all the notice Mr A's boss had taken of the Jerusalem and Jericho country they might as well have been in Fulham. Then he suddenly had this change of heart, or so it seemed. They'd strolled down to the water's edge, and Mr A was wallowing in time past and half-expecting Dan and Beersheba to come round the corner hand in hand, when the old man said, 'This place does something to me, it happened the last time I was here.' And Mr A's hopes were raised, and he said, 'Yes, sir?' And the old man said, 'Yes. All the goodness seems to go out of my underpants elastic. I think it's because we're below sea level.'

In the circumstances, of course, uncontainable fury was ruled out, and it's made Mr A more touchy with other offenders ever since.

Like the man at Lisbon. Or off Lisbon, rather, because we were sitting there in the observation lounge of a cruise ship one night, when everyone but us was ashore for free wine-tastings and little cork souvenirs. It was very quiet, and the moon was up, and there's a king-size gold crucifix that hangs in the sky over the Tagus just there, groovy Portuguese flood-lighting that blacks out the plinth and leaves the top bit. It's an experience, and beats the Captain's end-of-cruise cocktail party any time. Then this man bursts in with a buddy, holding an exciting surtax discussion. 'But you want to do what I do,' he yaps, joining us at the window and putting his espadrilles up on Mr A's footrest – 'keep your wife's shop separate, see? Different assessment and everything.' Mr A kicked his feet off and stormed out, leaving me to explain that he had a mild form of Parkinson's Disease that lost him control of his legs. Still, you don't mind that, to keep a loved one happy, and at least the taxmen stayed well clear for the rest of the trip, so that was something: just threw frightened looks and dodged behind a ventilator.

Unfortunately he'd already had one bout of UPS, coasting into the Bay of Naples, and I'm not afraid to say that I'd failed him that time, not wishing to roll up on deck at four in the morning to catch the view by dawn's early light. He went, though, and I'd hardly dozed off again before he was back in the cabin, shaking badly. I somehow diagnosed UPS as soon as I saw his stricken pan: the marriage bond, if still unfrayed, will often twang at both ends like this. It appeared that two lady passengers had also risen betimes for the treat, and beaten him to the prime spot in the bows to see the Bay. He'd have accepted that as the luck of the draw, like any good cruise-goer who knows there's only one place in the sun for any two contenders. What got him was that they were leaning with their backs to it, and no view but a stack of deckchairs under a tarpaulin.

'And guess what they were talking about,' he said when he'd taken a slug of Scotch and bicarb.

'If you thought I could guess you wouldn't ask me.' I wasn't unsympathetic, but he'd slumped on my foot and it was no time to mention it. 'I'll have a go, though. Carpet-shampoos?'

'They were comparing all the other cruises they'd been on – '

'What's wrong with – ?'

'I dare say. But not in terms of how many cheeses you get on the dinner menu. I bet you didn't know we've only got nine on this old tramp? They said they'd never dropped below eleven so far. The cows.'

We still had six days to Tilbury, and it didn't look as if I'd get him out of the cabin on any of them in his present state, in case he heard someone speak lightly of Amalfi cathedral, or take Hannibal's name in vain. Not that he knew much about either, but that wouldn't matter. So when his pulse was safely down in the mid-seventies I had to give him a bit of a talk. Darling, I said, people have to take their fun as they find it, you have to remember that, darling, Ow! would you mind getting off my foot, thanks. If all they want from Venice is group photographs on the Rialto bridge in paper hats with 'OK Tonite' across the front, how would he change things by having his coronary before its time?

The great danger with the fireside type chat is getting to enjoy yourself and going too far, telling them they've got quirks of their own, such as refusing to be on the over thirty-fives diving-for-spoons team, or trying to play 'They'll Never Believe Me' on any ship's piano recklessly left unlocked, and then looking wounded because everybody goes on talking as if nothing's happening. Which it isn't, of course, musically speaking. But only wives already measured for a strait-jacket would go that far. So I left his character flaws out of it. Just suggested that he hadn't dug out his bank account like a Stilton so that he could skulk below decks filling in the O's on an old ship's laundry list, while Stromboli went smoking by on the starboard beam, and he agreed eventually to come topside again. There's not much you can't work by touching them on their money's worth. I had to scout ahead for a couple of days, peering round the superstructures, but he never saw the cheese fanciers again. I think they must have slipped in from the first class, past a sleeping sentry.

You've been to Sounium, of course? That was what –

Q. No. But *does that mat-* ?

– what one of Mr A's educated friends said to him when we came back from Greece last time. You can have this sort of bad luck, picking an audience on your first day back from anywhere, when you're packed to the seams with anecdote and adventure. Some of them, you can hardly tell them what flight you were on before they're reeling off all the things they bet you missed when you got there. What, never saw the Hittite pudding stones? Missed the shrine of Theobald the Stiff? Passed within inches of Chopin's home-made rowing machine, and didn't eat gula-gula eggs by moonlight? You don't need much of this to wish you'd stayed in Hounslow and saved the money. In the case of Mr A's friend, who was a man called Willson Tiddly, two l's, two d's, and too awful, really, and that's about the only comfort to be had out of him, it was Sounion. Mr A said we were just —

Q. *On a matter of orthography —* ?
A. *It's a promontory, as far south as you can get. The temple of Poseidon —*
Q. *Thank you. It's just for accurate note-taking. I thought you said Sounium the first time?*
A. *Right. And Sounion the second, because I want to give the court a choice. It could be Sumion next time, and even Sanium, you never can tell. The trouble with the Greeks is this relaxed approach to place names. It's like spelling Newark Wenwrak, or Chigwell —*
Q. *Yes, yes. Thank you. I —*
A. *The Greek sailors —*
Q. *Exactly. Please continue from where you left off.*
A. *Which time? Tiddly, Poseidon, Chigwell or the Greek sailors?*
Q. *I've got Tiddly.*
A. *The court mustn't tempt the witness.*
Q. *I beg your —*

Actually (said Mrs A), if you did get Tiddly he'd probably give you the spelling of Sounion in the original, and you could settle for that. But you wouldn't have to mind if he flayed you for going to Corinth and missing the Canal. The way Tiddly told it, to see Greece — particularly Athens, which is only a bus ride off — and miss Sounion, exposed Mr A as an idiot and blind fool, the sort of stigma he can't wait to purge, if that's the treatment for stigmatism. His first chance was two years later, which also happens to be two years ago, by a curious trick of chronology. It was mine, too, of course, being a non-earning wife with a limited mileage radius, bounded on the north by Marshall and Snelgrove, on the south —

Q. *Mrs. A, please. Let's try to avoid the stream of consciousness. Perhaps if I*

*just ask why you have elected to depone on Sounion at all it would assist with the
direction of your statement?*

Because when we finally went there it was as near disaster as a
man and wife can get in a strange land, short of being dragged off an
Intourist luxury coach in Sverdlovsk and dropped down a salt mine.
What made it worse for me was that he didn't realize it. And someone
had to tell him, guess who. The Tiddly affair had an unusual effect, for
Mr A. Drove him to the indexes of Greek Myths and Legends, under
S, wherever they might be found. He may have missed a bit of stuff
here and there, in indexes where it was actually under Nousium or
something of that kind, but the result was that he got extremely
starry-eyed and lore-choked for weeks before we were due to go,
and by the time we went he was talking about Poseidon and Zeus as
if they'd all been at school together.

We didn't actually stay in Athens, owing to our balance of pay-
ments having a pinkish shade that year. We roughed it for thirteen
days in an unspoilt fishing village near Tiryns, which was so unspoilt
that the black-frocked grannies had their bath by walking fully-
clothed into the sea and holding on to boats while they bent down
and did their feet. There was one motor-bike, and as far as we could
make out it was purely recreational – the proud licensee just used it
to ride along the beach bisecting washed-up jellyfish, so it was all
very restful, really, not to say cheap. I tried to interest Mr A in Tiryns,
as the classical bug had got him, told him it was mentioned by Homer
and all the inside stones were supposed to have been polished to a
fine gloss by sheep, but he hadn't read about it, so compared with
Sounion it hadn't established itself. He just kept reading bits out to
me, as we drew our legs off the sand to avoid jellyfish particles, all
about Poseidon being the son of Cronus and Rhea, and having an
affair with his sister Demeter when she was disguised as a horse – you
got that sort of carry-on in those days, of course – and the Greek
sailors seeing Sounion as a sort of White Cliffs of Dover whenever
they came steaming in from bashing up Xerxes – and about the
temple on the headland, with Byron's name carved on one of the
pillars, and right underneath it, Bert Collins, Brookmans Park, and
many more. I don't mind telling you, by the end of the fortnight I
couldn't wait to see the blasted thing and get it over with. And the
ironic thing is that when we finally got there we never did see it.
Looked at it, but didn't see it. Because I'd told him about the disaster

by then, and we had other things on our minds besides the fact that you could stand up there and see Delos, Mykonos, Naxos, Paros, Andros, Tinos and Patmos, and the actual water Agamemnon sailed on.

We'd come into Athens the day before we were due to fly home, and this was Sounion day. Sound the trumpets. Willson Tiddly's hour was come. Owing to the fact that Cosmic Travel hadn't told us we could have come in by bus for fifteen bob, we'd had to hire a nine-pound taxi, from a garage just across the road from Homer's Tiryns, where they were always listening to football commentaries on the radio. We'd got a cheap bed for the night from an advertisement in The Times that had been yellowing in Mr A's wallet, an English girl married to an assistant sauce chef at the Athens Hilton called Kostopoulos, who let off the spare room to add an honest drach to the sauce takings. The taxi ran out of petrol somewhere outside Megara and the man got out, laughing, and disappeared on foot, finally bringing a couple of cans back riding on a road-laying machine, so by the time he'd found the Kostopoulos apartment, which he couldn't do until we'd given him the letter confirming the let, we only had time to fling down the bags, don a quick sight-seeing costume and leg it for the excursion coach. About all we saw of Mrs Kostopoulos, except for good afternoon-we've-got-to-rush, was a scream from a top window and a latch-key hitting me on the ankle in case we wanted to be late back. All very informal, compared, I mean, with the Athens Hilton. Speaking merely from supposition, however.

No sign of disaster so far, as you'll notice. We rolled along by all those sun-drenched Athens beaches, Mr A babbling about Zeus and Byron and Agamemnon and Willson Tiddly, and the female guide telling us how many planes a day took off from Athens airport.

'We'll be off from there tomorrow,' I said to Mr A. 'Have you got the tickets?'

'Tickets, please,' said the guide.

'Parakolo,' said Mr A, handing them over.

'Thanks very much,' she said, her English beating his Greek to a pulp, as usual.

'Now she's got them,' he said.

'The plane tickets,' I said.

'You worry too much,' he said. It's a line they love to take, when you're half killing yourself watching the little details that are their responsibility anyway. 'They're at Mrs Kostopoulos's, with all the gear. And a damned good riddance. You get stuffed with documents like a briefcase on these jaunts,' he said. 'It's like a happy release, having nothing but the clothes I sit down in and a hundred drachs for ouzo. Tell me, now, let's see what you remember. What was Poseidon the god of, darling?'

He might have been the god of foam rubber for all I cared, but I thought I'd better not say so. In fact, on the way to his temple I got more answers wrong that a street quiz on African politics. That old chill had got me.

'Why don't you relax and enjoy yourself,' he said, when we disembussed for the usual long craggy upward climb. 'You've got a lost look.'

It was a cue, but you save a lot of trouble in a marriage by making sure you've got a fire before calling the brigade. I let him have a good look at Byron's signature, also Bert Collins and many more.

'My God, what a view,' he said. 'When you think that the Argonauts, with Jason at the tiller – '

I don't know why the Argonauts should have touched me off.

'Where,' I said, 'is Mrs Thing's letter?'

'You have to remember that the Golden Fleece – '

'Did you get it back from the taximan?'

'Who cares? I wish you'd think about the ancient Greeks, you're wasting this whole thing. Try to imagine Menelaus, sailing in from – '

'I expect Menelaus knew where his luggage was,' I said.

'What's that supposed to mean?'

'What's Mrs Kostopoulos's address?'

'You had the letter.'

I'll hand it to him. In the circumstances he didn't take it half badly. We left the main party, which was being told that Poseidon used to be portrayed in old sculptures with a thunder-bolt, but later it became a three-pronged fish spear, and sat on a rock beside an ancient Greek litter bin.

'Have you got the Times ad?' I said.

'No good. Box number.'

'Did you see the name of the street?'

'What do you think? All I know is that it had a good view of the Acropolis, because it said so in the ad.'

'It had an Av. at the end of it, I think.'

'Rubbish,' he said. 'Sorry. What I mean is that a Greek Street isn't going to end up with the English abbreviation for Avenue.'

'It was An.,' I said. 'Short for Anastasia.'

'Look,' he said, 'there's bound to be a perfectly simple way out of this, if only we keep our heads. The cat at the hotel was called Anastasia, it had kittens under the reception desk. You've got your wires crossed. It had an Odos in it, though.'

'It would have, wouldn't it? Odos being Greek for street. There was a word at the end of the address, a district, like Clapham.'

'If you're trying to tell me there's a bit of Athens called – '

'Something like Bouzouki.'

'That's the music they play in the bus,' he said. 'Moussaka, was it?'

'Sort of cheese pudding. I think it was Koukaki.'

'Pure invention,' he said. 'Overstrain. Talking of buses, they're all going down. Catch the guide and ask her.'

'Ask her what?' I said. 'How to find a flat with a good view of the Acropolis belonging to an assistant sauce chef? What do you suppose the population of Athens is?'

He said he thought about two million, but we could ask her that, too.

It turned out, as you might expect, that the guide was a good deal more fluent on Tickets, please, and three-pronged fish spears that she was on finding addresses with nothing more to go on but the names of hotel cats. She admitted to a bit of Athens called Koukaki – one up to me, but it wasn't a time to score party political points – and the rest was old Athenian shrugs, and sheep-dogging the stragglers for the off.

We didn't say much on the way back, except that Mr A mentioned, about halfway, that it was getting dark. It wasn't a spirits-raiser by any means. Conceivably you could walk the city by day and hope to recognize a particular block of flats. By night the chances slimmed.

She stopped the coach at the Temple of Zeus and put us out, I don't know why. As good a place as any, I suppose, for a couple who didn't know whether they wanted Camden Town or South Kensington. It was beautifully floodlit, the Temple. Lovely. As if we cared. The only other illumination was car headlamps, about six lanes in both directions, driving fast, with hooting. Talk about finding the flat. We thought at first we weren't even going to get across the road.

'What about the tourist police?' said Mr A.

'All gone home, this time of night. Even if we could find them.'

'And if they hadn't, and we found them, what should we tell them?' said Mr A. Then he suddenly give a little yip. 'I'm a fool,' he said.

'No.'

'That key she threw down had a tag on it.'

'Tell me,' I said, while he was angling it to catch the headlights. 'What does it say, because I can't stand the suspense.'

'We shall only have to show it to a taxi driver,' he said, peering. 'It says "Acapulco Hilton".'

Gradually, as we wandered, we debated the possibilities. Phone the hotel in the unspoilt fishing-village, tell them to get hold of that morning's driver, explain that we'd given him a letter, and that if he hadn't chucked it away . . . All in Greek, of course. Or we could ring up The Times, ask them to go through their old Personal columns . . . We began to get a bit morbid after an hour or two. We liked Greece, but we hadn't intended to settle there, begging our bread. Would our friends and relations miss us? Miss Tweeley, next door, had only taken on the goldfish for a fortnight. What would the gardener say, turning up every Saturday and finding we still hadn't done his weeding for him?

Occasionally one of us would have a fresh burst of initiative, and say 'Koukaki?' to a cab that happened to be pulled up empty at a red light. They all answered civilly enough, and at length. Then drove off. Mr A even tried 'Moussaka?' with one, but he drove off without answering at all.

It was about half-past eleven that we collapsed on two kitchen chairs outside one of those dives that are trying to be a cafe but not quite making it. We ordered two ouzos, and I said to the man, 'Koukaki?' He wrote down on a bit of paper, 'Twelve drachmas'.

There was nothing to do but give up hope, and just as we were giving it up I saw something rather peculiar at the end of the street. A flashing sign saying Express Dairies. And not even in –

'I've heard her tell this about sixteen times,' said Mr A, entering with a hungry look. 'What about some lunch? And, every time – '

' – not even in Greek. I thought at first it was just an exhaustion symptom, a mirage. But when I told Mr A – '

' – every time, without fail, she says Express Dairies instead of Express Cleaners. However. When she told me – '

'When I told him I thought it was an exhaustion symptom – '

'I said no, it wasn't, because I could see it too. And she also said that she could see – '

'All right, all right,' said Mrs A. 'I know it's agony for you, anyone else holding the floor. You tell it.'

I'm only telling it (said Mr A, with charm) because when she tells it she doesn't do herself justice. No, I mean it. Whether it was dairies or cleaners isn't important, I'll give her that, actually. What matters is that by sheer feminine intuition, a commodity that many a husband scorns, but I personally would be pleased to take a bath in any time, she saw something else. I didn't, because it was round the corner out of sight, and if you don't put that in the extra-sensory perception class you aren't the court I took you for. 'Round that corner,' she said, screwing up her eyes in a way I always think not unattractive – it's all right, darling, you can thank me later – 'Round that corner there's another sign, saying Delicatessen. And round *that* corner – ' And suddenly she got up and ran. Amazing. After the day she'd had. I ran too, but I couldn't have done, without a pace-maker. And she was right. Round the corner past the delicatessen was the block of flats. She'd remembered, right down in her beautiful little subconscious. Never hear a word against Freud and Adler, is what I say. What's more, and I think it's my place as a husband to come right out with this, it was in the Odos Anastasia all the time, wasn't it, darling? That was what the An. was short for.

Q. *Just to clear up a minor point. I take it that you were able to establish the necessary ascendancy over Mr Willson Tiddly?*
A. *I'm sorry you asked that. Even Mrs A never asked that.*

'Tell me now,' said Mrs A. 'I'm interested.'
'It amounts,' said Mr A, 'to a slight negation of the whole Sounion expedition, I'm sorry to say. Still, if you insist. Yes, I saw him the week after we got back, and I said to him, "You'll be glad to hear that we saw your precious Sounion this time". And what do you think he said? He said, 'I don't know why you call it my precious Sounion, I've never been near the place. I just know that if you're in Athens, it's the place you're supposed to go."
'And what did you say?' said Mrs A.
'I should prefer to hand it up to the court in writing,' said Mr A.

IV

'Mother, I cannot mind my wheel.'
Walter Savage Landor

———————

WHEN we got back last Monday afternoon (said Mrs A) he went straight to the garage and sat in the car before even taking the bags into the house. I could see him there, when I came to prod the leaves out of the kitchen drain. Just sitting. Completely happy. Hadn't even got the radio on. And if I could give a message to world motorists through the medium of your columns, it's this: as the road fund licence doubles each year and petrol creeps up to a pound a pint, they shouldn't feel too disheartened about being priced off the road for good. To hear them talk, you'd think that when it finally happens there'll be riots in Parliament Square, with massed wrist-slashing and other signs of dismay and resentment. Well, they'll be sorry, if you ask me, because it could be the dawn of a golden age, when all the frustrations of actual driving and parking have been wiped away, and nothing remains but the pure spiritual joy of owning the blasted thing. Anyone who imagines it's the motoring itself that besots them –

Q. *Engrossing though the witness's thinking is on these matters, could we nevertheless* – ?

– should have been with us this last fortnight, that's all I can say, slurping up the kilometres somewhere between the Lot and the Pyrenees in a little tin box he never once passed so much as a rag over during the whole trip, and abused continuously in a deep hum I thought was engine trouble for three days but daren't say so. You wanted to ask something?

Q. *Simply to mention that my original question concerned the matrimonial stresses of Continental motoring, but I fancy you may be coming round to that now. Good. However, if the car was in the garage while you and Mr A were slurping up the kilometres* – ?

A. Quite right.

Q. Yet it was a motoring holiday?

A. Noticeably.

Q. Then how could the car be waiting when you got back home, for Mr A to go and sit in it?

A. We didn't take it.

Q. I – this is all – er. You didn't, I see. No, I mean. Could we perhaps – h'm? Yes. Does it strike you as hot in here?

A. I'll ask the ques – I'm sorry. It's all these courtroom dramas. Well, we could have stayed in the garden, only we should have heard Mr A banging the dishes about through the kitchen window and we obviously need all the concentration we can get. Why not a short adjournment for the court to compose itself . . . ?

Q. Mrs A. Just in your own words, please. How did you go on a motoring holiday and leave the car behind?

I was hoping (said Mrs A) that you'd be able to draw a simple inference without having it drawn for you, if you follow me. When I said the bit about passing a rag over it, not even to remove the foul-language film, it could have only have meant it wasn't his car, wouldn't you say? It's true he's taken his car before now, but it has this character flaw. It's an AA member. Alcoholics Anonymous. Drink the travel allowance dry before it had staggered further south than Rouen. In any event, even in the liberal old days when you could afford to watch its petrol gauge falling like an iced thermometer, it didn't make for the holiday of a lifetime. We only had to run over a dropped peach and it was stop engines, hard a-lee, and out in the road with the damp cloth and Karsheen before the juice corroded his hub caps. His idea of an early start to visit Vimoutiers and see the statue of Marie Harel who, as I needn't tell you, is reputed to have perfected Camembert cheese, was to be out at the back of the hotel for two hours before the rain came on, freeing his tyre treads of flints and bawling up at the bedroom window to know the French for hosepipe. This year we couldn't afford its thirst, and had to leave it in its garage. He was much grieved. He did his best to explain to it about the gnomes of Zurich, and how even cars that had done nothing wrong had to bow to them. It was a very moving scene, and he did well to tear himself away at all. Right from his parting caress and the doom-laden clang of the padlock, to last Monday afternoon when he could get back and sit in it, I could feel the bond between them stretching like fine nylon.

53

The hireling, or mercenary, was waiting at La Baule airport, with all its controls on the wrong side and a man from Nantes who didn't understand the English for 'Where's the hooter?' Mr A's impatience got off to a good start in the end, when he gave the man up for an idiot, slammed himself into the car, looked for the steering wheel and found he was in the passenger seat. It was an experience he kept repeating the whole fortnight, and it's a measure of my devotion that I always looked away when it happened, so that he wouldn't see me seeing him climb out again and crawl round to the proper side. Of all words best struck from the marriage vocabulary, the word gloat —

Q. *Ah! It was a rented car?*
A. You've got it.
Q. *Will you please continue?*

— leads all the rest. I don't say, mind you, as far as the preservation of the marriage goes, that motor cars haven't a lot in common, particularly in foreign parts, whether they're big old brutes practically qualifying as heirlooms, and enough man-polish-hours invested to lay the keel of a ship, or little bouncy boxes up to the door handles in ox-droppings. From a wife's point of view they both work out like home motoring only worse. But at least when you're grinding round Dorking or Roehampton you don't have to grip a bottle of Beaujolais between your knees with its cork rolled under the seat, and the end of a lovely long crusty French bread loaf in one eye, and the man at the wheel yelling, 'You've got the town plan, for God's sake, do we or do we not turn up this Boulevard Maréchal Jean-Pierre Sainte-Beuve into the Avenue du 4 Septembre and if you don't hook these plastic beakers out of my foot pedals we'll be clean through the Jardin des Plantes and up the Préfecture steps.'

Insecurity, that's all it is, of course, and a wife who wants to stay one has to remember this and make allowances. As she doesn't feel all that secure herself, stuck sideways in the middle of the Limoges rush hour, and he can't get the gears in because he's actually using the hand brake . . . or he takes off from a petrol station stinging all over from the price per litre and enters what's going to be the oncoming traffic stream as soon as a bit of traffic comes on, and she has to choose between a scream that puts him in a pumpkin field or that steady, low, flutey 'Don't you think we ought to be on the other side of the road . . . ?' Control, control, and again control.

Betty Weems stuck it out thirteen days of the fortnight last year, and was in sight of the winning post when she went off with a terrific bang in a direction that surprised even her. Thirteen days and nights, she went, and the more Willie Weems got insecure about the roads, the hooting, food prices, and signposts saying 'Au Château' that led down overgrown dead-ends that he had to come out of backwards, the more she gave out with the controlled, 'There, there, my darling,' and 'What does it matter as long as we're together,' and the like. Then on this last night, simply because, she told me afterwards, he wouldn't take any of her map-readings, just navigated blind to show who was wearing the trousers around here, they had to put up in the place they were finally lost at when darkness fell.

It was one of those hotels, she said, that your friends are always stumbling on – look absolutely nothing, but when you get inside it's got this smiling service, beds like floating in gossamer and a proprietor who was Chef for twenty years at the Crillon, and so anxious to get his hand back in with the poached turbot and shrimp sauce that he'd do it free if he wasn't afraid of insulting you. Actually, the one the Weemses stumbled on not only looked nothing, it was nothing, they had ants, no plumbing, and a dinner of tinned peas, vulcanized veal and a cardboard apricot tart they wished they'd taken upstairs to wedge the window with. And Betty was sitting behind the dirty little oilcloth curtain with her feet in some cold bidet water out of the hot tap, reading the Michelin by a fifteen-watt bulb – but at least it hadn't a shade, so that was a help – when Willie suddenly yelled out, 'What the hell are you doing in there, eating some private food you've smuggled up? Come to bed, can't you, I've had eight hours' driving today, it'll be nine hours tomorrow, and if you think that blasted ferry's going to wait while I catch up on my sleep in a lay-by you're a bigger fool than I took you for.'

'Coming,' she said. Holding on still . . . only twenty-four hours to go.

'What are you doing?'

'Just looking up tomorrow's route, darling, that's all.'

'Going to get us bloody well lost again, are you?' said Willie.

'I don't think so, darling.' Very low and flutey. 'You just drop off, there's a good Willie.'

'Drop off?' he said. 'Drop off? And you coming in here threshing like a giant tuna the minute I've gone into shallow breathing? Just let me tell you something – '

'No,' she said, coming out with her suspenders dangling. 'Let me tell you something. Your legs stink of garlic. Thirteen nights I've slept with those stinking garlicky legs, and between you and me iast night was the last time, OK?'

She said Willie sat straight up in bed with his jaw dropped. Couldn't even utter, let alone pull himself together enough to sniff his legs.

'Oranges, too,' she said. And she took her bathrobe, also the peg, being that sort of hotel, and went down and slept in the bar. The last I heard of her she was living with a married sister in Malmesbury and Willie in and out of the lawyers ever since, working on the restitution of conjugal rights.

Tragic, really. I mean, everyone knows that fourteen days' car picnics are a strain, when you can't squeeze enough funds out of the Treasury to get more than one knife-and-fork meal a day, and it probably wouldn't have happened if Willie hadn't insisted on driving in shorts and sandals with his knees for a table and always letting Betty have the only three inches of hot bath water – ironic in itself, when you come to think. I keep advising her to take him back. She established an ascendancy in that one speech that a lot of girls work right past their silver wedding for. She could have a lot of happy years with him.

It's well known, of course, that the car picnic is at the bottom of a lot of broken Continental holidays, especially if you're renting the car over there and can't squander baggage weight on your barbecue kit. Picnicking in the homeland reaches high standards of sophistication these days, come a long way from the squashed tomato sandwich and banana, and on a fine weekend a lot of car boots are better equipped than an Ideal Home kitchen. With those al fresco snacks on the side of a motorway, which seem to appeal to so many people's urge to get away from it all, you can lay out your chairs, tables, cooker, hot plate, ice bucket, finger bowls and probably a couple of small waiters from Ring and Brymer's. Or take a night at Glyndebourne given that the rain holds off: out you come in the interval, discussing whether you've been seeing *Don Giovanni* or *Figaro* – because it's the food and drink that's important, there – spread the snowy napery, drape your pearls on the hock bottle, pass round a lordly dish of quail's feet in sour honey, and generally have such a ball that you decide not to go back inside. But mewed up on the drowned banks of the Loire it's different. Those little hired cars aren't only short on space, they haven't any flat, level surfaces. Balance a mug of coffee on the average arm-rest and you've got your handbag full in a flash. No one realizes the wealth of tilt they build into a seat-back these days until they've left a lump of salami on it while they reach down to scrape some chutney off their foot, then it's down inside the back of your dress like a nose-bleeding cure. Even if the sun shines it's no better. There aren't any flat, level surfaces outside either. The car we had this year sloped off in all directions, like a seal. Possibly with plenty of time and a slide-rule you could have found the dead centre roof spot where a bottle defied gravity for a second or two, but we never did. We lost a whole cheese in a wood outside Bourges. Only a small one, but it was the main course. Didn't find it until Mr A wound the window shut and it came up with the glass. No, all you can say for the car picnic is the occasional new flavour experience. How else would you hit on seedless grapes and mustard?

Still (said Mrs A, smoothing a reminiscent wrinkle) the thing about the Weemses' blow-up was that it didn't really have to be car picnics at all. Holiday stresses are cumulative, so it's when you get to the last couple of days that a marriage enters its explosive period and any spark can do it. And I mean any. Florence and Weedy Harrington survived a whole fortnight in Sicily a few years ago without a blow being exchanged. Even sitting in the plane at Palermo, waiting for take-off, they were still on speaking terms. Then Florence dropped her guard for a second. Over-confident. Beckoned Weedy's ear over and yelled above the jets, 'We never saw any bandits.' Flash-Bang. He took it as a slur, and went up his in mushroom cloud. Had she the faintest idea what this holiday had cost him? Didn't she damned well know he'd rather stay home and get in some multi-track tape-recording than career all over Europe flinging purses of gold everywhere right and left? The whole blasted trip had been for her, anyway, and if she now had the crass, grasping, stupendous, female gall to start beefing about the bandit shortage . . . ! Florence said afterwards that if they hadn't been half down the runway by then she'd have had to get the Captain to him. But there again, the bandits were only a – what's the word, starts with an animal – ?

Q. *Catalyst?*

As you say. She could have asked if he'd remembered to pack the eucalyptus and set off just as big a bomb; opened up his secret grievance about always being the one to get the mosquito bites, while she went the whole fortnight without a puncture. In fact,

I've just remembered, it was mosquitoes that split up the Garforth-Smythes, only the other way round. This was in Rhodes, I think. She used to wake up every morning absolutely distorted all over with bites, but they didn't fancy him for some reason. It was all right for a day or two, while his sympathy stocks lasted. He even offered to change beds, but the mosquitoes changed beds too. Then at the end of the first week he suddenly looked up in the middle of his what-do-you-call-its, vine leaves stuffed with rice, and said in a low, tense voice, 'If you're going to scratch, darling, just come right out and scratch, do you mind? What with trying to get your chair-back under your shoulder blades and going round all the table legs playing the 'cello with your ankles I haven't tasted a thing yet, it's like sitting opposite a family of pythons.' She was out and up to the bedroom in half a minute flat, including a good scratch waiting for the lift. And glad to go, actually, because there was a sharp-cornered wardrobe drawer up there that was bliss for bites in the upper lumbar region. But that didn't stop her testifying later that he'd called her a python in a public place, and they got their separation the following spring.

Q. *If we could keep this particular statement to the influence of the motor-car?*
A. *Certainly. Please scratch if you want to, by the way.*
Q. *Thank you. Yes?*

I'd make the point (said Mrs A) that a great hazard of the motor-car is the detour, anyway, but I'm pleased to wrench my evidence back on to the main highway, or route nationale, with the rather distressing case of Gerald and Mopsy Queenbridge and their tour of the chateau country that finally blew its stack at Le Touquet.

They were a couple you'd see at a bar and form a snap character judgment that couldn't be more wrong. He was one of those calm, or po-faced, men with hairy bowlers and very clean shaves, who look as if they'd take over the lifeboat drill when the ship's sinking and the crew are all to pieces in the scuppers. Actually, he'd just got to look like that on his national service and it didn't mean a thing, because inside he was sentimental, insecure and still believed the pictures on the seed-packet. And you'd have been just as wide of the mark with Mopsy, one of those fragile little china blue eye batters you wouldn't dare ask the way to the post office in case she dissolved and ran through the paving cracks. It if came to it, though, she'd be the one to take over the lifeboats, and probably end by chucking the ship's band into the last boat one after the other, still playing 'Nearer, my God, to Thee'. Pressed steel infrastructure and leather organs, she'd got, under all that flutter and bubble-cut. And it's a funny thing about couples, if the court doesn't mind a slight pronouncement here, but the people they marry usually turn out to be other people not long after the knot's been tied, and I often think it's peeling off the layers, and finding stuff you never thought was there, that keeps a lot of marriages going just on suspense alone.

They'd been dogged by the seed-packet effect the whole of that holiday. They'd never taken a car abroad before, and Gerald hadn't ever been to France. Just knew it was full of girls with frilly garters and little striped hat boxes, and the first gay cafe awning you sat under there'd be Gene Kelly dancing on the tables. He got more and more wistful during the two hundred miles they drove on day one, looking for that cafe in the great northern plain, and they had to settle in the end for an ironmonger's with only one table outside and a window display of Daz packets, in a village that wasn't even on their Continental AA route, and seemed to have been cleared for flooding under a hydro-electric scheme. It wasn't a good start, especially as all they could get was Nescafe, and a packet of biscuits labelled 'Uncle Sam's Genuine Pocahontas Crackers'.

'Where's the Loire?' he said, an hour or two later in the middle of some French Stoke-on-Trent, where ten thousand workers were going home on bicycles.

'Keep right, past the chemical factory,' Mopsy read from the route.

'Where are the Châteaux?'

'Left after the cement works,' she said, 'and past these abandoned barracks, it says, and in three miles we come to something with an asterisk, see back . . . "Fine spiral granite staircase, sole remains of the Château Puypelisse, now standing in grounds of psychiatric hospital". Should we go and look?'

'How many steps?' said Gerald, his upper jaw muscles working like a horse with the shudders.

'It doesn't say. Why?'

'We could run up them and jump off.'

'Now, now,' said Mopsy. 'Anyway, it says apply to physician in charge for permission to visit, July and August only. Why do we keep going round and round this railway goods yard?'

The more you want a thing, of course, the less you're likely to get it, we all know that, and it probably had a lot to do with Gerald's disenchantments to come. His first meeting with the Loire wasn't too good. He'd kept pushing on past various side roads down to the river, either because they had arrows saying 'Le Camping', and he said he wasn't driving eight hundred kilometres to see a lot of tents full of Northampton hairdressers, or – and this is the old trap with personalized transport – because he always thought the next one would open up a vista fit to knock his eye out. It could have done with it by this time because it was getting moist with disillusion, and although Mopsy was keeping her leather and steel in reverse so far she thought she'd better mention that the road and the river were now diverging, and if they didn't want to find themselves at somewhere called Meung they'd better dive down the next gap and enjoy themselves while they could.

That was how Gerald got his first glimpse of French rubbish. They came out on to a grit foreshore bright with bottles and crumpled kitchen foil, but a few old boots and broom heads took the glare off and there was a touch of colour from strips of gingham blowing in the brambles; also a few dozen empty ten-pound tins, labelled Haricots Blancs au Naturel. Mopsey thought of trying to distract him with a fantasy about peculiar Gallic rites held at that spot, where the locals met by the new moon to throw their clothes off and eat beans. But she wasn't sure it would take, the stricken way he was looking, so she suggested they strolled down to the brink of the fabled waters, where they'd doubtless see ten or eleven châteaux reflected in the limpid depths. Not so. Whether it was some sort of plot specially laid on to upset Gerald she never found out, but they seemed to have more or less drained the river at that point. What was left of it was oozing sluggishly between long, low grit-banks like a school of gravel-backed whales.

'Crying won't help,' she said, supporting him back to the car. He was one of those men whose emotional distress induces physical failure, and she had to lower him on to the smoothest boulder she could find before he was strong enough to hold an egg-sandwich. 'You have to remember,' she said, 'that even old Father Thames isn't all Hampton Court and Henley. Besides, we've at least found a place that nobody else has.' Bad luck with that one, too, because she was still saying it when a flock of French widows driving tractors and trailers came roaring down off the N.152, hemming in the car on all sides and starting to shovel flints. Even Mopsy wasn't up to an explanatory fantasy about this. In any case, she was too busy yelling, 'Over here, over here!' so that Gerald could get a fix in the dust cloud.

By the time he was equal to leaving it was nearly dark. This was one of those late season holidays, hoping for cheap rates and the pick of the bedrooms, but it often means pressing on into the deepening gloom looking for your dream hotel, and in the end grabbing whatever's going, which in the Queenbridges' case was a single room for two overlooking a fairground – and Gerald mysteriously bleeding from the upper right thigh. They found in the morning, after paying double Michelin rates because, as the Madame explained, the room they had wasn't built until after the Guide was printed, that he'd sat on his sun glasses. Things were really piling up now. Mopsy tried for the bright side over the sun glasses, pointing out that it was raining, anyway. It wasn't a big success. I think that was the day they got the car stuck in a farm gateway, up a track they shouldn't have been on, trying to see a château they never found.

Still, it wasn't all gloom, don't think that. When they hit the Resistance country Gerald perked up quite a bit at the tragical-romantic aspects. He took to stopping the car and standing bare-headed outside little houses with crossed tricolors over the door, and the words, 'Honneur à l'Elu'. Hostages, he said. Terrible. Just think . . . the tramp of jackboots . . . villagers picked at random . . . put against a wall. Honour to the Chosen. Oh, yes, the French might squeeze you until the pips squeaked and take the bath-plugs away, put the châteaux where you couldn't find them and keep Gene Kelly and the frilly garters under wraps, but they'd certainly done their bit for the Peace, and you had to make allowances. It fed his sentimental needs for the inside of a week before he poured out all these deep feelings on an English-speaking barmaid in Roc-Amadour. If Mopsy had been there she could have stopped her, but she wasn't. She told him he'd got hold of the wrong end of the stick: what 'Honneur à l'Elu' meant, in a roughish translation, was 'Best of luck to the newly elected Mayor and Councillors'.

It hit him very hard indeed, and there were more blows ahead, such as setting the town plan of Limoges on fire with his new electric car kettle, being ordered up a cul-de-sac in Brive by gendarmes and kept there all afternoon while a six-day bicycle race went through, and finding that the son-et-lumière they'd driven sixty miles to see at Chambord had done its last show of the season the night before. Mopsy began to wonder if she'd get him back to Woking in his right mind. She blamed herself for the Chambord fiasco, what's more: she should have remembered sitting with him two years before, under an Athenian moon on top of the Acropolis. The *lumière* was OK, that time, but when the English *son* struck up, in plainly recognizable voices from the BBC Drama Repertory, Gerald was fit to be tied. He hadn't expected personal appearances by Demosthenes and Themistocles, he said, stumbling blindly down the slope, but Carleton Hobbs and Rolf Lefebvre were pushing it a bit far.

So it was time to take over. Cut the romantic losses, was Mopsy's proposal, one day towards the end of the second week when Gerald was well anaesthetised with Grand Marnier; make it back to Le Touquet the day before they were due for the air ferry, and beat the place up in a riot of unconfined flesh-pottery that would make a Roman orgy look like a reading circle tea. Gerald concurred. It wasn't just that he knew when those hoops of steel were closing: when you've given romance every chance of playing along, and all it's come up with is gravel-trailers and six-day bicycle races it's time to quit for the ankle deep Aubusson, crystal chandeliers and a reception desk you can hardly see through a foyer-ful of uniformed Peke-walkers.

'You're on,' he said. They'd got four hundred francs held back for emergencies, and if the need to lose the lot at the tables wasn't an emergency he didn't know what was. 'Best five-star hotel in the place', he said, reviving with a jerk that surprised even him. 'Beakers of the warm south all round the clock, and what the heck if they have to wheel us to the airport on a barrow. Let's start now.'

'Well, say first light,' said Mopsy, midnight now being within striking distance. But she had to admit that, for the first time, it all looked a lot more hopeful.

The miles went fast next day, whiled away with talk of the high life to come. Gerald said that before they even booked in anywhere they'd get seats for the best show in town; it might be hard to make a decision, with a feast of nighteries like that but never mind. He said he felt like a musical, himself, and if the worst came to the worst he'd even settle for something he'd seen before, like Oklahoma or Kismet, provided they'd got big enough names. He hoped the casino had a cabaret. You could only look at green baize just so long.

That whole day's motoring he only had two setbacks. The first was at a small, flyblown restaurant in Gournay-en-Bray, where he ordered a pâté billed as the chef's special, and was well away before Mopsy noticed. Of course, she should have kept her trap shut, but when nerves are strained to this pitch a girl can have lapses. 'And you a nature-lover?' she said to him, hardly thinking. After that she had to go on. He was on his last mouthful of toast then, but when she showed him the menu and told him the English for grive he left it on the side of his plate. 'You mean I've been eating mashed-up thrush?' he said, going a mid-slate colour. 'This damned country. I'd noticed there weren't many birds around. Show a beak outside the nest and I suppose you're whipped in the pot.' However, the incident didn't take the toll that Mopsy had feared, at any rate then, and they were about twenty miles short of touch-down, turning left into Neuville, before he clouded over again.

'What's up?' said Mopsy, sensing that he'd slumped inside his shirt.

'Suppose,' he said, 'the five-stars won't let me in the dining room with no dinner jacket? Settling for a four could cook the whole thing.'

Mopsy gripped his arm with a vice-like reassurance that nearly had them off the road. 'First man to lift an eyebrow,' she said, 'and I'll break both his legs.'

'Fine,' said Gerald, knowing she could do it, and put his foot right down.

It was Mopsy who smelt death in the air, even before they rounded the last bend. The terrible, waxen stillness of a short-season resort with all the shutters up. The beach was printless and bare. The Boulevard de la Plage, blood-soaked in the low evening light, reeled away before them as empty as a derelict air-strip. Traffic lights winked their idiot sequence of red, green and amber, and no car to care but theirs.

'Not many people about,' said Gerald. 'Ah, there we are!'

A dying ray was glinting on the words CASINO THEATRE, with a cruel mimicry of its erstwhile neon. In Gerald's mood of exultation it was enough to fool him. She let it. The reckoning would come, and that soon. At first she couldn't look at him when he came back to the car down the broad white steps, having rattled the locked doors and gazed in stupefaction at the empty display frames.

'What the hell's going on? *The bloody place is shut!*'

'I think you'll find,' Mopsy said, 'that everything's shut.'

She told me that she absolutely hadn't a clue how he'd take it. She was prepared for anything. Even so, he still surprised her. He hadn't got back in the car. Suddenly, on the pavement, he bent completely double. She said he kept his legs straight and put his face between his feet, but you can get exaggerated images at a time like this. Anyway, it turned out it was terrible pains in the stomach. 'It's the mashed-up thrush,' he whispered.

Psychosomatic, of course. But that doesn't make it any better if you've got it. She folded him up in the back of the car and scoured the whole of Le Touquet, from the blank, closed five-star seafront to little half-built roads running into the sand at the back. Eventually a poor old mad woman took them in and gave them a bed over a fish shop, under the impression, Mopsy gathered, that they were distant relatives from Quebec. The room had a wallpaper with a tiny butterfly design, and Gerald, when he wasn't being sick, swatted it through the long, dark hours with his sponge bag.

You've heard of people's hair turning white in a night. This is what happened to Mopsy's liver, perhaps the only case of its kind. When Gerald was well enough to start telling her how diabolically she'd failed him, which she thinks was about 5 a.m., she found to her amazement that she hadn't the steam to utter. Just sat there, taking it. It must have been a terrible experience, for a girl who'd reduced people like bank managers and stationmasters to a mere tremor before now. The last time I saw her she still hadn't clicked back, and I don't think she's bothering now. She married a high-class Suffolk taxidermist who only stuffs rare animals. It's rather uncanny, really, because he's not unlike Gerald to look at, only in his case it's not a false front. He really would take over the lifeboats. Mopsy's finding it very restful, I think. And if you saw them together at a bar your snap judgment wouldn't be all that much out. I mean now that Mopsy's more or less what she looks like, too.

Q. I take it, Mrs A, that this is an entirely true story?

A. So I've been given to understand, yes.

Q. Yes. I see. And, just for the record, what happened to Mr Queenbridge?

A. Just for the record, I suppose you won't believe it, but he's married to a big games mistress and English Ladies hockey goalie named Rosemary Tough. She is terribly insecure, apparently, and needed a real iron man to lean on. So, of course, if you saw them together in a bar —

Q. Yes. Thank you very much, Mrs A. As I seem to have more than usually elaborate notes to write up, would it suit you if we adjourned half an hour early just this once?

V

'And where thou lodgest, I
will lodge.'
Book of Ruth

———————

IF I could just make a small point (said Mr A), I wouldn't want
anyone to think this is a marriage with a nine-room villa at
Santa Margherita and we're stuck out there six months of the year
to beat the buff envelopes. Actually, we're stuck here fifty weeks of
the year and have to get out of it for the other two in order to
preserve a balanced view of the Government, the pop scene, the
mounting flood of apologies over the railway loudspeakers and
other aspects of the human predicament, if the phrase doesn't
strike you as extravagant. It doesn't? Oh, good. And even then it's
always a bit of a debate whether we go away at all, or apply the funds
to getting the outside of the house painted. As you probably
noticed when you drove up, we've been away about ten years
running now, and one of the front windowsills has recently collapsed
under the weight of a thrush. Then again, there's the movie-camera
aspect, with its misleading suggestion of high living. But if you've
ever watched a coachload of Californians unloading at Versailles,
all with two Bell and Howells apiece and the leather casing alone
worth its weight in Bethlehem Steel holdings, you'll realize that I
wouldn't dare unwrap mine from Mrs A's tartan suntop until they
were safely round the other side of the Petit Trianon sorting out
their arclights and zoom lenses. I picked it up very cheap in a street
market just off Holborn Viaduct, and even then it was some time before
I could afford a second-hand projector – a very frustrating period,
that.

It's just that if your notes got left in a cab and fell into the hands
of the means test people I wouldn't want them to bracket me with
the Gettys and the Gulbenkians as a man who always knows where
his next yacht's coming from. Without being in the least disloyal to
Mrs A, an admirable helpmeet and no fool in the kitchen, she has

E   65

this proneness to drop the occasional snob place name, which is more important to a girl than a lot of men recognize.

Q. Yes. I take it that a mention of Santa Margherita is in order?

A. Perfectly.

Q. The Parthenon?

A. Entirely.

Q. No objection to Versailles?

A. None. Or Le Muy.

Q. Oh. Should I know that?

A. Not if you can help it. The same goes for the nearby resort of X, as I prefer to call it, rather than get sued by General de Gaulle, his successors and assigns. Though I suppose even he couldn't exercise absolute power over the mistral.

Q. The strong, cold and dry north to north-west wind in southern France and adjacent areas of Spain and Italy, when the air sweeps south from the French central plateau and is funnelled through the Rhône valley to the delta, often blowing in a cloudless sky but reducing temperatures to considerably below normal for the time of year?

A. You could put it like that.

Q. Will you please go on?

Both my wife and I (resumed Mr A) are anxious to give evidence at some later sitting on the subject of the elusiveness of public conveniences in foreign parts, and often of substitute amenities of any kind. We consider that this is a matter the travel writers skirt round with chicken-hearted squeamishness, considering the permissiveness of our times and the universality of the problem. I should get that bit down in my exact words, if I were you, because the chances of your improving on them strike me as thinnish, all right? So I think we'd better keep this aspect of our visit to Le Muy until about section ten of your report. This doesn't mean that its other aspects can't be touched on at this time.

Our actual centre, however, was X, that year, and in fairness to my wife, whose selection it was, I must say that when the recommendation came in from Tom and Tatty Hewitt they were just back that day and it was rather late on at the Truepenny wine and cheese party, the time when you get undue garrulity on the one side and undue credulity on the other. You know how these things go. Words like fabulous and fantastic flying from the lips like cocktail onions – and cocktail onions along with them if you don't watch it. So, of course, practically the first I knew about it she'd booked two weeks at this fabulous resort with its fantastic rooftop dining room, private beach and a headwaiter called Emile who'd move heaven and earth for us at a mention of the Hewitts' names. If she depones, by the way, that she told me all about it and I just sat slumped down to my shoulder-blades taking no notice –

Q. *Yes?*
A. *Oh, well. I expect you're pretty good at assessing a witness's credibility.*
Q. *Go on, please?*

The trouble was that the Hewitts had been there in high season July. My wife fancied something a bit earlier, before all the bougainvillea was shrivelled up by the sun – because this place was up to the roof in bougainvillea, Tatty Hewitt said: you had to watch out when you threw the bedroom windows open to each new day's glorious vista of sea and sky, otherwise the stuff came bursting in and got shut in the dressing-table drawers. I have to admit, all the same, I didn't mind going in the low season that year, owing to having had new discs, exhaust system, clutch, tyres and a touch of panel-beating that winter. They'd actually got the car at the garage when we went, spread out like a heart transplant, otherwise we could have gone in it and things mightn't have taken the turn they did.

They say London's a fine place for people who can get out of it, and it was even truer for X. And we felt it more, I think, when we turned up in the old hired Citroën from Nice, with its front wings waving like the dance of the seven veils, and about six lots of Germans were just moving off in a motorcade of Mercedeses, the whole world their oyster. When our link with home went rattling and burping back towards the setting sun I felt like something I couldn't quite place. A little baby when they snip the umbilicus? Some chap put down in the Antarctic, and no one coming back for him until the year after next?

'What do you feel like?' I said to Mrs A, needing just that note of connubial empathy so helpful at such times. She said she felt like a large brandy, and when I thought it over I felt like one too. And the mistral had hardly started then. It was in the middle of the night, I think, that there was a clump on the front of the hotel which can only be likened to a giant hand, and the wardrobe doors flew open. From then on it never really let up until the day we got back to the airport. Then it was such a flat calm I didn't think there'd be enough puff to lift us off. Mrs A, largely owing to inexperience and simple faith, has none of these apprehensions about aeroplanes. Always nips the 'For Your Safety' leaflet out of the little net pocket in the back of the seat in front while we're waiting for take-off, has an enjoyable read about life-jacket knots and when to remove dentures by numbers. Myself, I'd rather die completely smiling, if it came to that. Fortunately we're both pretty well-molared so far, but what with the rising expectation of life these days, and all the chemicals in the food, bridgwork at some future date obviously isn't to be ruled out, and I suppose it depends on how you see the sudden end of a happy marriage. Locked in each other's arms, just smiling at the back and sides, hardly seems the – What did you have for lunch, by the way?

Q. *I beg your pardon?*
A. *I think I reversed the eggs and the milk proportions in my omelette. I get these rather sombre states of mind when the stomach's lined with excessive albumen. Excuse me.*
Q. *Not at all. I take it your wife –?*
A. *Quite well. She didn't have any.*
Q. *In any case, I hope to take evidence later on in the field of transport, when these matters might drop in better. Would you care to continue filling me in on X?*

It's as near as you can get to the French Riviera (continued Mr A) without paying out real money, though the word real is relative, because after the first week's bill we had to cut back severely, even on the Vichy, Vitelle, Evian and other bottled conspiracies to conserve French hotel tap-water. Luckily, whenever the wind dropped a point or two, we were sometimes able to make it to the village drinking fountain and quaff a few copper cupfuls on the rates.

Even during the first week we'd kept well on the right side of actual intoxication. The first three days it was curiously difficult to catch the eye of the barman, and on the Thursday, of course, this organization called the Leicester and District Friends of France arrived in force and caught all the eyes that were going. It was a pity about the barman, because it looked very much as if we were going to be thrown on him for the social side, in lieu of headwaiter Emile. We'd been banking on Emile more than we realized, following the Hewitts' dazzling testimonial.

'Ah, Emile,' we said to him at dinner on the first night – 'have the the kindness to accept our assurances of the most good remembrances

68

from Tom and Tatty Hewitt.' He responded with an instant recommendation of the lobster, twelve francs extra, not in fact being our contact at all, who turned out to have quit at the end of the previous summer. Probably his back was killing him after being bent double all round the clock for those benighted Hewitts and he'd taken it off to Lourdes. His replacement was a refugee from Salonica called Athenasiades Igoumenopoulos, and somehow we never got on name terms.

We didn't get what you'd call really close with the barman, either, because he was permanently on his hunkers at the back of the bar, where he had intensive duties connected with running water. Even by the end of the fortnight we never really solved it. He kept squirting the stuff into various sized tins. You could hear they were various because some filled quite fast, up in the coloratura in no time, and the others went on drumming away for ages in the tenors and baritones. He was no slouch at this work, because we never heard one of them run over, and this meant constant repositioning, as far as we could make out, rasping the full ones over some sort of specially echoing tiled floor he'd got there and shutting them in sliding cupboards with doors that banged like guns. Then he'd slide some more doors back, bang, bang, bang, get fresh tins out and off you go again, not a second's pause, like handbell ringers.

The best answer we could come up with was that some dam had sprung a leak, up in the mountain at the back, and it came down clean through the hotel, and he was keeping it at bay until they could get an engineer up there to seal the crack. We managed to have a chat with him late on the third evening, I think it was, when he'd got all his work battened down for the night, and was easing his spine against a stack of wine bins, but it seemed rather early days to ask him what it was he kept piddling about at, quite apart from the language barrier. However, we managed to get some information out of him, also the loan of a chess set, which he kept in what seemed to be a tea-chest full of old James Bonds and Agatha Christies with the backs off. Mrs A, I have to state entirely off the record, if you'd care to down ball-points a minute, tends to lose her sense of priorities when it comes to fringe packing. Squashy plastic bottles of sun oil have their place in the cosmic scheme, no doubt, and the same with inflatable beach beds, chunky rubber bathing caps and gaily striped robes of coarse towelling. Also sentimental old 10-lb. chocolate boxes wedged full of rare tropical remedies, throat sprays, crêpe bandages, athlete's wrist-straps, rejuvenating unguents and every kind of exotic nard –

Q. Exotic – ?

Nard. For bracing any suspected slackness at the back of the ear lobes, smoothing away unsightly shin-freckles, and the like. Of course we all have our blind spots, and I suppose she doesn't see the uselessness of this equipment for people pinned in a small wickerwork bar with no entertainment but the dribbling tins, the howl of the force nine and an exhibition of paintings by a local amateur filling all wall space with random explosions of solid colour entitled '300 fr.' on little labels on the frame. What's needed in this case, as any packer of imagination should realize, is all the board-games you can muster, not even excluding backgammon. To be fair, though – you can quote me again now, should the occasion arise – we shouldn't have had the fun out of our own chessmen that we got out of the hotel's: this was short three bishops, five pawns, two knights and the white queen. As we had to make up the gaps in the ranks with lumps of sugar, potato crisps and little black olives it was quite frolicsome at first, bagging a potato crisp bishop and crunching him down. Then the novelty wore off, notably after I'd run out of olives and had to use a sleeve button. 'That pawn tasted funny,' I remember Mrs A saying, and then we realized.

That was when we were brooding on the information from the barman, which was mostly negative, viz., that he couldn't say when the mistral would stop, it could last a fortnight. He was correct to the day, as it turned out. That they'd opened the vaunted roof-top dining-room on the Monday, as a five-minute experiment, and all the striped umbrellas had sped off like a flight of arrows for Corsica. Also, that the private beach would be available in due course, but at the moment the bulldozer levelling the drifted shingle had been blown on the rocks, and the driver was on strike for danger money. Eh bien, etc., there was nothing against having a shot at the miniature golf round the back, if we were roped together and one of us hung on to a strong tree, always supposing anyone could find the clubs. And yes, indeed, véritablement, and so forth, the long, luxurious, south-facing, beflowered and vine-clad suntrap of a *terrasse* overlooking the limpid Mediterranean, as mentioned in the brochure, was indeed out there awaiting our pleasure. Anyway, it had been this afternoon, he said. Cependant, and the like, you wouldn't get him trying to serve any drinks on it in prevailing conditions, not unless – and I'm afraid this is only a rough translation – he was first handed the medal of the Legion of Honour, wrapped in a sworn undertaking to look after his next of kin.

It was the next morning, Thursday, that the Leicester Friends of France came coaching in, singing. Or it may have been Leeds. They'd been down the coast somewhere attending a big town-twinning fest, or similar excuse, and were now booked in solid at our address for a three day's knees-up and chips, before buckling down again to the footwear and hosiery business, or, if Leeds, cloth, chemicals and cellulose. Their spirits were high, and by rights, of course, the sound of English laughter, and the sight of thin blondes in gold pants being chased in and out of the little coffee tables by agile light-engineering executives, should have lightened all hearts. It didn't work like this for some reason. Even on their last night, when they took over the bar for farewell speeches and a number of presentations, mostly crocodile handbags, we never really chimed in with them. And it was the first shock of impact, on this Thursday, that drove us to try the terrasse anyway.

It wasn't a success, largely because we hadn't a set of weight-lifter's bar-bells to hold us down. There were moments of interest, as the occasional blue streak of Gaulloise packets flashed by, keeping low for Yugoslavia, or a passing beret struggled for a moment in the railings before dwindling to a dot on the south-eastern horizon. Nothing really came out of it, in fact, but a sharp scream from Mrs A, with a hand to her cheek. Flattened there was a yellow bus-timetable, or horaire – a word I can never remember when I want it, but that's bi-lingualism for you – and it brought home to us the need for a change of scene, which is what a holiday's for, I always say. It's never been cleared up why my wife picked on Le Muy for the big breakout. She –

'You picked on it,' said Mrs A, backing in with a tray. 'Because you hadn't the guts to risk asking for two returns to Draguignan.'

'It's never been cleared up why my wife picked on Draguignan. She – '

'We didn't go there, so it doesn't matter. This is the first non-teabag tea we've had for a fortnight, and not with hot condensed milk either. Darling, make a bit of room for his cup between those socks.'

'My wife always comes the educationist, trying to make me speak

71

the language. Considering she's always bringing home little imitation snakeskin carriers of Linguaphone records – '

'Once. And they were Greek.'

'What's the Greek for Good Morning?'

'I'm afraid there's no cake,' said Mrs A.

'There you are, you see. Yet when we wanted that bus back from Sparta – '

'Sugar?' said Mrs A. 'He loves dropping the snob place name.'

' – she made me spend the morning working out the Greek for 'Will you oblige me by reserving two seats on your sixteen thirty-five hours service for Athens, not under the canned music loudspeakers'. Then I queued for half an hour at the bus station, rehearsing it like a rune, and when I got it out pat the man said – '

'They like you to speak their language.'

' – the man said, "Today or tomorrow?" in very good American English.'

'You couldn't have been all that pat,' said Mrs A, 'otherwise he wouldn't have booked us under the canned music loudspeakers. No one who hasn't looked death in the eye over five hours of mountain hairpins, with non-stop bouzouki perforating their eardrums – '

'Perfectly ordinary bus ride with a very good driver. Just because you thought the old woman in front was gasping with fear at the bends, when it was only the vacuum brakes – '

'Good driver or not, any road where he has to wear a little wash-leather apron to stop the steering wheel sawing through his waistband . . . And who was it said at the end, "My God, I'm glad to be out of that, my legs are like jelly"?'

'You're thinking of when we – '

'Besides,' said Mrs A, 'he had more ikons and votive-lights and little crucifixes strung along the inside of his cab . . . '

'She's thinking of when we walked down nine hundred and sixteen steps from a Venetian fortress.'

'It's hard to have full confidence in a man who can't see out of his windshield for protective charms and amulets, including, in this case, portraits of his dead parents, three footballers and the Holy Family. Though, I must say, I'd rather see it in a bus than on an aeroplane flight-deck. When we took off in the car-ferry from Lydd last year, my husband daren't even – '

'Before you say anything you might be sorry for,' said Mr A –

72

'I'm told that any depositions about transportation are slated for a later session. And you were the one, if I remember aright, with the jelly legs.'

'Try and make it stand up in any court, that's all. By the way, did you know one of your film reels is unreeled all over the scullery floor? I've tried not to tread on it much.'

Q. *Your husband was about to give me some evidence on Le Muy. I wonder if you would care to carry on in his stead?*

We were under-documented, as usual, that was the trouble (said Mrs A). Timetables are OK, but you really need a map to go with them. My husband had this idea that if we got a bus going along the sea-front, it would keep going along the sea-front, and as long as it wasn't blown off the road we could sit back and enjoy constant panoramic views of the storm-dashed cliffs, so it didn't matter much where we were making for, provided he could pronounce it and there'd be food and drink at the other end. It was naturally a bit disappointing when we turned sharp inland after about half a mile, and enjoyed constant panoramic views of abandoned farm houses, derelict breweries and a whole mountain range of used-car dumps – the sort of thing the authorities probably discourage in the hinterland of the Riviera proper, but here it looked more as if they'd just declared it a distressed area and left it at that. It wasn't the impression we'd given our friends at home, when they'd said where are you off to this year, then, and we said, oh, just the South of France, you know, little suntrap near Cannes, nothing very exciting, just flopping out on the sands with a tall drink, and them saying, fabulous, you lucky old things, poor old us, we're stuck with the Trossachs again. These thoughts can weigh on you, grinding on through a series of French Sloughs, with the occasional stack of old tyres burning in the deserted fields. It weighed on Mr A particularly; for one thing, because he's very romantic under his rugged exterior and thinks he ought to be able to put his hand out of the window of any French bus and pick a passing grape; for another, it was his first year with the movie camera and apart from a few shots of wind-bent palm trees and men in blue trousers battling about with their heads down, he hadn't got a thing in the can, and thought this was going to be the day for his big Côte d'Azur travelogue. Actually, all he got for the whole trip was the sequence of me coming out of the Gents on the football ground, which I made him swear on his honour to chuck in the dustbin.

73

You probably don't know Le Muy. It doesn't get star billing in the French guidebooks, in fact it doesn't get a mention unless you've got something very comprehensive, with large-scale maps that practically mark the water-hydrants. As it happened, we found we had got one of these, when we came back, and although it was a bit short on anything to say about Le Muy itself, except pop. 2128, apparently something pretty exciting had happened about two miles off in 1536, when a man was shot in mistake for Charles the Fifth, whoever he was. Mr A was livid when he found this out: he said if he'd known at the time he could have photographed the approximate spot. I pretended to be sympathetic, but it's his own fault for messing up the packing; he always says, never mind the guide-books, we can always get them at the other end and save weight. The same with games. I'm always for a bit of precautionary scrabble or cribbage, but if I put them in he only chucks them out again. 'Good grief,' he said last time, 'we're going to be spread out like starfish all day, with the vitamin D running out of our ears, and you know what you're like after a dose of sun – hardly carry your lipstick back to the hotel, let alone sit up all night playing two-handed Monopoly.' I don't know where he gets these ideas from, but it doesn't do to try and dislodge fixed thinking. Many a holiday marriage has come back and taken cabs in opposite directions, just because the husband insisted he could tell squid from octopus and the wife wouldn't let him get away with it. That's what finished the Dawson-Weekeses after Majorca. They started an argument in the underground lakes at Porto Cristo about whether stalactites hung down or stuck up, and by the time they got home, with the chance of taking it to arbitration with a dictionary, they'd forgotten who'd been arguing what; just knew that they'd got a war to the death with its origins obscured by the mists of history. It's very (said Mrs A) sad.

I used to try and make Mr A read the guide-books before he went. Not a hope. Then I tried to stop him reading them when he came back. No luck there, either. He hasn't got around to them yet this time, but it's going to be murder in a day or two. Luckily we're not clean out of tranquillizers, in spite of the bumpy flight back, so as soon as I hear him yelling, 'My God, do you realize we went clean through this place and never saw the statue of the Comte de Valbelle's wolfhound,' or, 'Why didn't you tell me there was a hole in the ground where the Huguenots stored silkworms' eggs', I shall swallow one down and wait till it's over for another year. Mind you, I can see

74

the frustrations. As Mr A always says, when he's reaching the cooling-off period, you might as well not travel at all if you come back from Ravello not knowing that Flavio Gioja invented the compass three miles off in 1302. And talking of compasses, Bert and Poppy Duckworth got lost in Pisa and never found the tower. They separated for nearly a year on that, then it was patched up with a stroke of genius by Poppy. She had a tax-loss boutique in Worthing by then, so she got a business allowance to buy Italian silks, swearing on her application form that Worthing wouldn't look at any other sort, and invited Bert to go along as her secretary. Actually, they had a frightful row when they saw the tower. Bert was disappointed because it leant less than he'd been led to expect, and Poppy wouldn't go near it because she thought it might be its day for finally falling right over. It's dreadful, really, when you think you can get incompatibility over degrees of lean, and they only stayed together again because they realized how they'd both missed a year's bickering.

In a way, though I must say I never thought I should hear myself saying it, this is all making points in favour of the guided tour. You may have to cram into a limestone grotto with forty Swedes and listen to a lecture on pagan rites, but when you get home afterwards and find Colonel and Mrs Fiske were there the year before, at least you don't have to stand blushing like fools while she bawls across a roomful of people, 'Julian, you won't believe this, they were at Puque du Roi and never saw Richelieu's boots.' Or the Roman drains, or whatever it was.

One thing about a place like Le Muy, it only needs a mention and you've got the Fiske types fried. They say they don't know it, as if it can't be up to much if they don't, but at their heart's core they're quaking with one-downmanship. Anyone can bandy Villefranche or Ogliastro Marina, probably just got them out of Godfrey Winn's autobiography, but bandy a place like Le Muy and there's nothing for it but to ask for details. That's when you come the wagged finger, say it's your own little secret, and the last thing you want is to have it trampled flat by a tribe of Fiskes.

It's not easy to give you details of Le Muy, actually. Think of a deserted Spalding, if you know Lincolnshire at all. With gusts of plaster-dust blowing, and what we thought was a dead dog in the middle of the street until it went for Mr A's trouser-cuffs. I saw it as some sort of accident of planning, round about the time William the Silent was assassinated. Someone found a tree there that only bloomed on the centenary of Joan of Arc's birthday, something of that kind. They ran up a few quick huts for pilgrims, with picture postcards and any relics they could pick up cheap, then it struck them there'd be a hundred years to wait before the cash rolled in, they turned to other things and the scheme folded, leaving behind a sense of purposelessness and, as of a later date, a closed radio shop where the bus stopped.

I can admit to you, though I'd keep quiet about it in the ordinary way, that I was pretty pleased with this imaginative reconstruction, and if I couldn't get Mr A interested in it, that was just jealousy – and he was also in low heart, of course, with the whole adventure to date. His own theory was that we'd arrived in the middle of some frightful dark crime in which the whole village was involved, and Maigret would be along any time now, stripping off layers of deceit behind the closed shutters and uncovering horrors fit to put his pipe out. I thought it was over-fanciful, myself, but I didn't say anything. He'd had another rather gloomy setback, somewhere around the last car-dump but three, when he worked out a bit of French asking the driver which was the best hotel for lunch. We hadn't seen the place then, of course. I suppose it was like asking a Huntingdonshire busman to reel off the five-star listings in St Neot's, and all he did was tell the rest of the bus about the request, causing them to laugh uncontrollably for about the first time in twenty years by the look of them, and in some cases actually let go their chickens.

However, when we turned up outside the radio shop the driver nodded across the road to the Hotel Boule d'Or opposite, which was obviously not only the best, but the worst and only. It was also where the plaster-dust was coming from, being largely under construction, or perhaps just being shored up against collapse.

Mr A, who was having a touch of the Boswells that year, writing all the menus down, didn't even get his notebook out for that one. We concentrated on the wine, which I warned him was asking for trouble, but he wouldn't listen. He said even the Boule d'Or must have toilet amenities, and I'm bound to hand it to him, when we'd each put away three-quarters of a bottle he came right out and asked two yellow-looking men sharing our table where it was. Considering his trouble with the bus driver it was very heroic, even if – not in any way to diminish his achievement, you understand – he was under some pressure. However, where it was, it turned out, was in that part of the building taking the main brunt of the demolition, and our two friends were demolishing it. Their yellow look was plaster-dust, and they got up and went into a back room and continued their devil's work. I think we can call it that, in the circumstances.

With the meal over and three hours to bus time we tried to raise each other's spirits by saying that even the residents of Le Muy must be subject to the basic natural need. But after several surveys up and down the street, by which time shutters were opening suspici-ously, there was no sign. If I can put it like that. What's more, there seemed to be some local by-law against deserted side streets, alleys of any kind, little shrubbery-studded gardens –

Q. Excuse me. I wonder if – ?

– or any access to the back of deserted properties, themselves in good supply. If there'd been any sights to see it might have been an answer. Even in backward areas it's accepted that a coachload of pilgrims, making their first stop since lunch –

Q. Would it be possible – ?

– can't get a real kick out of the tombs and reliquaries unless – Still, both Mr A and I could gladly make a fuller statement some time, under this head. Nothing draws –

Q. May I just ask – ?

– a marriage closer than a common goal, so it's very much a rele-vant subject, if that's what's worrying you.

Q. No, no. I quite accept that. I was only going to ask – ?

And absolute frankness can't come too early, that's another thing. An open covenant openly arrived at, and the wife making it clear, right from the start, that the popular fallacy about girls being able to – Where are you going? Oh, I'm frightfully sorry (said Mrs A), it's straight across the hallway, little white door on the left. I can't think how I could have been so thoughtless.

VI

'To where, beyond these voices,
there is peace.'
Alfred, Lord Tennyson

———

THE camera's been a godsend in its way (said Mrs A, curling up on the sofa in a nest of badly-folded road maps). Not enough girls make allowances, in my opinion, for a man's toy-complex, the way he misses the fun of taking the back off the grandfather clock, or assembling the occasional do-it-yourself bookcase, and I'd advise any wife to remember this, if she doesn't want to find herself deserted on a dune at Deauville. Any summer's day you can see beaches full of deprived husbands, marooned on some foreign strand with nothing to do but catch sand-flies in a matchbox, wondering how to drop a hint about getting back three days early so that they can rip out their record-player deck, blow into the works and put it back on again. Sometimes it comes on them even before they leave home, especially if they've got something new that they've hardly played with yet.

A case in point, because I know you people are crazy on documentation, was Eileen and Trev Trotter, the first married holiday they had. Naturally, it was left to her arrange it. It came as a bit of a surprise to her, as a matter of fact, because her best friend had a husband who spent fifty weeks of the year up to the scalp in Continental AA routes and the French for brake-lining, so that they could spend the other two weeks stuck in the Pyrenees waiting for a propeller shaft to be flown out. She didn't realize he was a freak. The general run of husbands take the view that the weaker vessel, with nothing to do but sit with her feet up and let down last year's hems, is well placed to plough through the travel supplements and pick out the ideal Shangri-La. Trev Trotter was no exception, and Eileen spent most of their first year in a riot of sun-drenched brochures, trying to fix him up with a Costa Brava tan at Broadstairs prices and some snob place names to drop on the 8.43, which is more important to a man than a lot of girls realize.

I forget where they finally settled for. Somewhere she could pronounce, like Normandy. I mention that, because the average husband
prides himself on being the pronouncing animal, when it comes to
place-names. He can be slumped down his Parker-Knoll up to the
shoulder blades with his eyes shut, while the little woman does
her nut with the guide-books, but she's only got to get her tongue
tied round places like Port d'Ourdissétou or Castiglioncello, and
he's down on her like a ton of Berlitz tutors. Funny, really – yet
what isn't, with them, when you come to think of it – because when
the time actually comes for a bit of vital fluency on the other side of
the Channel, he'll slip her into the Syndicat d'Initiative like a ferret
and take off for a quick stimulant at the nearest bistro.

Anyway, wherever she'd picked for him, she must have been on the
finalizing details, because it was while she was asking whether he
thought they could get away with tucking a little illicit folding
money into the emergency Bronco packet that she realized he'd
withdrawn from the debate, with his scowl in position and his vision
clouded. It's very frightening when they suddenly retreat into
transcendental meditation like this, especially in the early days of
wifehood before you've got your mind-reading diploma. But at
least Eileen kept her feet on the ground at first, diagnosing catarrh
and hardness of hearing.

'Have you gone a bit deaf, darling?' she said.

He was quite vehement, denying this. Eileen said afterwards, as if
she'd got a special case or something, though goodness knows she
hadn't, that he only had to have a lump on his elbow to be talking
about it twenty-four hours a day, whereas if she so much as remarked
on a wheeze in his glottis he went on as if she was making advance
plans to give his body to medical research.

'Sorry,' she said. 'What do you think, then?'

'Think?'

'Do you think they'd find them, at the immigration, if we slotted
a couple of fivers in the bumf' – pardon the Anglo-Saxon, just giving
you the reported speech – 'and made sure the interleaving still
looked factory fresh? It's smarter than folding them long and thin,
and pretending we didn't realize we were using them as bookmarks.
On the other hand, it's a dodge everyone else may have thought of,
in which case the Customs men go straight for the toilet paper like
a – Darling, you're still not listening.'

'Not what?'

'You don't want to go, do you?'

'Go where?'

This is when a girl's heart turns to gooseflesh. She's losing him. Everything they told her is true, after all. His first grand rapture blunted, he's met some different-shaped girl at a Harrogate trades fair, can't bear to be parted from her for a fortnight, and any time now he'll be asking for his freedom.

Eileen told me she hoped never to go through those terrible moments again if she lived to be a mother of nine. There she'd been, trilling on about breathtaking old backwaters and magical mountain grandeur, with bananas, flowers and fruit in abundance, and Trevor as blank as next year's diary, with his eyes fixed on the end of his slippers. Playing for time, she upped her voice half an octave and went into ecstasies over the recorded highlights of the Bergen Line's cruise No. 53, Bulken, Skanevik, Haugesund and Strandebarm, with an optional dash round Ibsen's birthplace, but her heart wasn't in it, and when she'd sailed right through the small type saying all tariffs were subject to alteration without notice she ran past the full stop and said Darling you would tell me wouldn't you I'd rather know the worst and get it over with than go dragging on like this.

'What the hell are you talking about?' said Trev.

'Is there someone else?' said Eileen.

'Don't be a damned fool,' said Trevor.

And naturally, at the tenderness of these words, her tears of relief burst forth on a scale fit to boost the water level of the Hardangerfjord coastline until the local Vikings started sandbagging the front steps.

'Now what are you crying about?' he said.

'I'm not crying,' she said, gushing like a hydrant.

'In any case,' said Trevor, 'I always thought bananas were fruit.'

'They are,' she said, knowing a well-intentioned change of subject when she saw one. Sniff, sniff, blow. 'Why?'

'You said magical mountain grandeur with bananas, flowers and fruit in abundance.'

So they both turned on the writers of travel brochures, and after that it was all kiss and make-up. And, believe me, a girl needs all the make-up she can lay her hands on after making a boob like that. Once a shaming old line like 'Is there someone else?' has rung around the domestic welkin you need to paint over the cracks and forget, while you can still live with yourself. So there was this –

Q. *If we could possibly recap a minute. I seemed to be –*

– happy ending, I'm glad to say. Admittedly they didn't actually go anywhere that year, but it tided them over until next year, and she loved him for making the kitchen radio trivet, even though they had to get a real carpenter in to fix the larder shelf back. And by next year, of course, Trev had his movie camera. That's a toy they can take abroad with them and only counts as hand luggage, if you're lucky, whereas a powered drill, with stripping, sanding and buffing attachments – You were saying something?

Q. *Thank you. It's just that I seemed to be following you very well for a time, but I'm afraid I've lost the scent now. What larder shelf, radio trivet and real carpenter? And what happy ending, come to that? Why was Trev – er – why did Mr Trotter – ?*
A. One at a time.
Q. *Yes, indeed. But these are merely supplementaries, Mrs A. I've already noted down a number of useful pointers in the matter of stress factors arising from vacational matrimony, which is my immediate purview –*
A. It is?
Q. *– even though I haven't got my first proper question in yet, viz., 'With regard to subsequent recriminations, is it advisable for the holiday venue to be selected by the husband or the wife?'*
A. Neither. Take the Hewitts. He was –
Q. *Hadn't we better – ?*
A. When Tom Hewitt decided –
Q. *Mrs. A. Please. Later. If we could first finish off the Trotters?*

'That's better (said Mrs A, removing a bottle of duty-free Rémy Martin in a sharp-edged box with coloured carrier string), I thought these sofa springs were going. Ah, well, now, I see what you mean. It's possible I skipped a bit of plot there. I think you'll find I was discussing toys a short time back, before the bit about the other woman came up.

Q. *I take it, by the way, that there was in fact no other woman?*
A. Certainly there was.
Q. *Ah. I'd got the impression – However, if you'd kindly continue?*

She was (Mrs A continued) Trev Trotter's mother. At the risk of teaching a matrimonial investigator to suck eggs, I'd say that the element of maternal intrusion is an ever present trouble in time of help, if that isn't stretching paradox to a point where I shouldn't bother to write it down if I were you. Your husband can be a great hulking personnel manager, greying at the temples, and what personnel manager wouldn't be, these days, but that doesn't mean his Mum doesn't keep his baby-curl folded in fine tissue with its source of origin written on the outside – as if she was going to stumble on it one day and go half out of her mind wondering what the heck it was. So naturally when his birthday comes round she's not going to let it pass as if it was just some meaningless April twenty-third, or whatever it happens to be. Trev Trotter's was actually in the middle of May sometime, which couldn't have been worse. They were planning their carefree fortnight away from it all to start the first week in June, and then these two men came into his life.

Q. I'm afraid anything in the sphere of consenting adults –
A. Black and Decker. From his mother, with many happy returns.
Q. Ah, good. Yes?

Well, there it was. He'd hardly done more than drill an old piece of skirting-board full of experimental holes round the back of the garage, and now there was this frightful prospect of being cut clean off, with agonizing withdrawal symptoms. So all the time Eileen was streaming on about the mediaeval magic of the Venetian Riviera he just sat brooding on the idea of having to waste the golden hours haggling with some money-grubbing gondolier, while his glittering new powered carpentry kit collected dust in the cupboard under the stairs. Anyway, I certainly hand it to Eileen, because he'd no sooner made his position clear than she took all the brochures down the garden and made a bonfire people saw two miles off in Epping, and the holiday period ended up with this lovely larder shelf and radio trivet. There were a few setbacks, of course, because he was still more or less in the testing stage. Bored clean through a gas-pipe at one point and was running round the place yelling 'Where have you put my stuff for sealing radiator leaks, for God's sake?' Then a lot of his other holes got in the wrong places, and the first time Eileen looked in the larder she thought he'd smuggled in a wall-sized Gruyère as a surprise.

There was a bit of a tiff when the shelf collapsed, too. He said she'd overloaded it. She said if a shelf couldn't take a pot of chutney and a bag of lemons without pulling its brackets out – well, I don't need to tell you. But apart from that it was one of the best holidays he'd had, he told Mr A later, especially when the hired carpenter came in to do the job right, and Trev could stand over him with useful tips and advice. The transistor trivet wasn't anything the Design Centre would have run up a flag for either, as a matter of fact, but there again Eileen came out of it well and kept telling him he was a clever old thing. It had two main errors of judgment, actually. He picked a bit of kitchen wall for it where it stopped the crockery cupboard door opening more than a foot, so that if she wanted a big meat dish out she had to sidle in backwards: and it was all length and no width to speak of. Their kitchen transistor was very directional, by a bit of bad luck, and of course there wasn't room to turn it round and beam it on anything the BBC was putting out. And she didn't want to wound him by not using the trivet, so about all the radio she heard for two months, until it fell out of the wall and he used it for practising powered screwdriving, was a lot of rather strangled, high-pitched messages from the Essex county police cars.

It's worth mentioning, while we're on about holiday toy-deprivation, that the transistor's as good as anything for a husband knocked off his drugs. It isn't only that he can sit on the banks of the Loire twiddling through the static for a voice from Home – and you'd never believe the thrill he gets, picking up road reports about a burst water-main at Uxbridge – but he's got this lodestone for his mechanical instincts, warped though they may be. He can prod around inside it, passing the hours away, and even if he busts it he can go on prodding, trying to mend it again.

The tape-recorder runs it a close second these days, of course, now that they've got the watchermacallits, batteries. Holidays were hell when they first came in, weighing the best part of a hundred-weight, and it was a choice between a husband's recorder or a wife's second suitcase, let alone the nerve-racking suspense all the way to Estoril, or wherever it was, in case the Portuguese electricity came out of the wrong plug-holes and blew its back off. Now a man can be happily spooling away all day, just as if he'd never left home, and come back wreathed in tapes of Turkish circumcision ceremonies, or genuine wails from the Wailing Wall. That isn't to say that the holiday wife hasn't to be understanding about it: she just has to realize that actual grown-up husbands are a figment of the male novelist's imagination; they all have what we call in married woman circles the Teddy Bear syndrome. It can be one of those wristwatches with winders all round like a ship's wheel, and a lot of dials indicating blood-alcohol levels, high tide at Westminster Pier and the proper depth to plant horseradish, or just a simple fixation on anything electronic. In any case, the really bright wife can't do better than bow three times and leave the room backwards. At least when she comes in again he may have taken the blasted thing into his work-shed for a spell of private communion.

This is one of the difficulties with toys on holiday. That's how Gwladys Morgan – Gwladys with a 'W' being from Aberystwyth – left her husband a year or two back – left him in a chalet-bungalow near Spotorno, playing his mouth-piano. Just scooped up her traveller's cheques and took a fast Trident –

Q. *Excuse me. Playing his – ?*

– direct from Genoa to Middle Temple Lane, E.C.4, Tracy, Tracy, Ramage and Hinch. Playing his mouth-piano. You must have seen them in the music-shop windows, baring their teeth between the guitars. She thought for a time that Dai's was a gift from a secret admirer or similar no-good tramp, but she decided in the end that he must have bought it himself, either in a mad fit of impulse shopping or a pathetic bid to recover his lost youth, when he'd had a short spell as substitute cornet with the chapel band. In either case you can hardly blame him for clamming up: a man of forty-four, and about the same round the pyjama cord, thinning up top and a prison visitor, doesn't want it spread around that he's trying to master the mouth-piano in his spare time.

It was unfortunate that the bug bit when it did. Timing can often be the whole trouble in these cases. The first Gwladys knew about it was less than a month before this take-off for Italy.

'You go up, Glad,' he said one night. 'I think I'll hang around down here and catch the epilogue.'

'The what?' she said.

'The epilogue,' he said.

Obviously it wasn't a time to go into a lot of ecclesiastical why's and wherefore's, so she just reminded him to put the milk bottles out and went up. I asked her, when she told me about it, whether she didn't get a touch of the green-eyed monsters when she hit the Slumberland, cocking an ear for the muffled click of the French windows and a bit of stealthy rustling. But no, it appears. She was just settling back on the pillow with a few weeks' arrears of colour supplements when she heard what seemed to be a musical sheep having a shot at the first line of 'God bless the Prince of Wales'. A few radar sweeps of course, and she got a fix, slipped into something loose, as it might be language, and went down and found Dai shut in the scullery, blowing down his little keyboard on line three, 'Oh, let the prayer re-echo'. Not if she knew it, she said. Once was plenty, and if the neighbours had an ounce of public spirit they'd already be dialling for the St John Ambulance, with panic messages about a strangulated hernia at 'Betys-y-Coed'.

Even so, things weren't serious at this stage. It was when they arrived at their individual type chalet-bungalow on the hitherto unspoilt Ligurian coast, and the first thing she saw when they unpacked was the mouth-piano, that she sensed the grim turn things were taking. She stuck nearly a week out, going long lonely walks along the sea shore, wearing earplugs at close quarters, and lashing up plates of spaghetti all around the clock – not that it would have sounded much different, she said, if he had tried to play with his mouth full. And she might have managed to stay the whole course, in fact, if one of the thing's notes hadn't gone. Dai had a theory that they'd poked about in it at the Customs and wrecked one of the reeds. It was wrecked, anyway, whoever wrecked it, and instead of playing Doh it went phurb every time. That's what brought things to a head. Small though those little private chalets are, she could just about have swallowed 'God bless the Prince of Wales' for a fortnight. It was 'God bless the Prince of phurb' that stuck in her gullet. I think I can say, and I'm not given to wild or extravagant statements, as I know you'll agree – I beg your pardon? Oh, I thought you said something – I think I can say that it's one of the saddest stories I know. They were a nice pair. Lots in common. Mouth-pianos excepted. Tragic really. And there were two other unhappy features of the bust-up, now I come to think of it. One was that if only she'd gritted her teeth and hung on, which is such a vital discipline in the married state, it never need have happened. Because by the time the Decree came through, Dai had entirely lost interest in his musical renaissance, and the last we heard of him he was doing further education classes in upholstery. Aren't I right, darling?

'Certainly,' said Mr A, who had entered with a tray of drinks, cheese straws, assorted cocktail sundries and dismantled projector parts. 'What about?'

'Dai Morgan, giving up music for cushion-stuffing.'

'I think he's on motor-bike maintenance now,' said Mr A. 'Or perhaps it's judo. In any case, I'm afraid we're very much to blame for the whole tragic business.'

'Exactly what I was going to say,' said Mrs A, 'before you came in and poured those very small gins.'

Mr A topped up extravagantly all round. It had not been his wish, he explained, that the investigation should start dancing and tearing the place up, or fall asleep and roll from their seats in a stupor, according to which way the stuff took them; and added, 'I certainly think you're right to make a clean breast of your responsibility in the matter.'

'My responsibility?'

'I hope you're not suggesting it was mine,' said Mr A. 'I'm off back into the cutting room. There's a great sequence of you, by the way, shot from below, when you were climbing the gate to get away from that goat.'

Q. *And now, perhaps, for the other unhappy feature, Mrs A?*

A. *The stuff doesn't burn these days, of course.*

Q. *I beg your pardon?*

A. *It's the modern obsession with fire prevention. In the old Mack Sennett days — not that I go back that far, and if you're writing this down I hope you'll underline it —*

Q. *Certainly. But with regard to the unhappy feature?*

A. *Any feature that has me escaping from wild animals in it is unhappy, for my money, ha-ha. Bit of word-play there, but never mind. I was just saying, if Douglas Fairbanks had run off a home movie of Mary Pickford legging it over a rail-and-post fence she only had to bung it into her Beverly Hills boiler and it was gone in a flash. Happy days. This goat-and-gate bit that my husband's so pleased with, I shall have to spool the whole film through, find it, chop it out and bury it. It could take a morning.*

Q. *Yes. Mrs A. If I might just bring you back — ?*

By all means. The thing that sticks in our consciences about Gwladys and Dai is that they wouldn't have gone to Spotorno at all if Mr A hadn't sent them. He first met Dai in circumstances that have never been cleared up, really – on a British Council brains trust laid on to teach overseas students about the British way of life. They'd only learnt about it from books, and asked such questions as what had happened to the hansom cab, and why the Duke of Edinburgh

86

wasn't King. I could understand Dai Morgan being on it, also the Irishman and the Scotsman, but Mr A was a mystery, and I can only think that whoever made the arrangements must have turned over two pages. Would it surprise you to learn that all this is by the way? Good.

There's something very nasty, I always think, about those cases where motorists give a lift to an old pal and have the misfortune to run into the back of a parked milk-tanker and break his leg in two places. The nasty part is that the old pal hobbles into the nearest lawyers and is out again like a shot to stick a writ on his benefactor's windshield. I may not have got the legal details right, never mind. You're constantly coming across this sort of thing in the headlines – 'Kindly Act Caused Bankruptcy', 'Good Samaritan Must Pay £17,500,' and so forth. And my feeling over it is that common courtesy's gone the way of the hansom cab. Even lifts to old pals are pretty much on the wane these days; you never know, they may have taken up cosh and grab work since you used to know them in the bank, or wherever it was. So when somebody actually does go to the trouble of braking at the bus stop, flinging the door open and telling you to hop in, the least you can do is take any consequences in the right spirit. Kindly acts are above rubies. The fact that you get out without noticing that the window-winder's in your coat pocket, and the leap for the pavement splits you all down the side seam, is not a thing to take any account of. What sort of a creep are you if you can't wait to call on him waving a receipted repair bill? Answer, you're the sort of creep that practically everybody else is, judging from those headlines.

And all this leads me, in case you were wondering, to the extremely dodgy business of holiday recommendations, and the extraordinarily few cases, considering the grasping modern attitude referred to above, in which Mr and Mrs X sue Mr and Mrs Y for recommending them to some island paradise where time stands still and nothing's changed since Alaric the Goth, and when they get there it's a mass of Bingo, bed-bugs and beach-photographers. I don't know, offhand, what it costs to set a double fracture to British standards in the average leg, but compared with a flopped holiday it must be negligible. Especially when it turns out to be the trigger for a flopped marriage, as with Morgan vs. Morgan, mouth-piano intervening. As a matter of fact, even if they'd sued, and put Tracy, Tracy, Ramage and Hinch on to us, instead of each other, I think Dai's musical addiction would have been a useful cornerstone in our case for the defence, on the ground that we knew nothing about it at the time.

Q. What time would that be?

Well, it would be a Thursday, because that's when I go to the hairdresser's and read those magazine pieces by people who've walked into the best hotel in Verona, explained that they represent a hundred and sixteen Thomson newspapers, and find to their amazed delight that they're made a real fuss of, impeccable cuisine all hours of the day or night, smiling service all ranks, every miniature-golf ball scrubbed personally, and the manager driving them to the airport in his own car when the long trick's over, after making a pleasing little ceremony of tearing the bill up. They don't mention the last bit, of course. They're professionals, those travel writers; they know the ordinary reader will have had his credulity pushed a bit already, considering that the last time he was in Italy he could only get a room with a broken bed light and no clothes-hangers, overlooking a bend on a steep hill where a thousand cars an hour revved, changed, hooted and screamed their tyres all night, and when he tried to get a nap on the terrace during the hours of daylight the chef's fat little daughter always joined him at the table, eating peaches out of a polythene bag and throwing the stones at bathers.

In the case of Spotorno, I think what took my fancy under the drier this particular Thursday was simply the idea of the individual chalet-bungalows. They've caught on a good deal since then, of course, and if ever you accompany us on our magic carpet to the fabled land of Crete, we shall have more to say about them – especially when they turn out not to be individual, but semi-detached, and your husband says, 'Hello, what the hell's the matter with this door into the other part of the joint, it seems to be stuck,' and a voice on the other side says drop dead, can't you, how are we supposed to get a bit of shut-eye in here.

And I can only think, reverting for a moment, which may suit you, I shouldn't be surprised – what happened was, when Mr A collected me and my brown rinse, I said, 'Who was it saying the other day their holiday had been wrecked by weddings?'

'Whose hasn't,' he said. Well, it wasn't my fault there was no parking outside Madam Potter's and he'd been making the rounds of the block getting his wits whetted. It's often best just to ignore these challenges to a verbal duel.

'I know it was France,' I said, 'because it was this French wedding. And raining. They watched it from the bar, began with a two-piece band, trombone and saxophone, and all the soaked relations dressed in black – '

'You've got to hand it to the French, they can show nice feeling.'

' – and it was a small hotel . . . it's coming back to me . . . with very cheap oysters . . . and most of it was let off for functions all the time. And they found out later that the wedding party was one of the functions, and the dining room was just under their bedroom and the laughter and song kept up until in four in the morning. Then the next night it was a farewell supper to a local gendarme moving three villages down the coast, and the night after that another wedding. Then I think it was the landlord's birthday, and after that – '

'Yes, yes,' he said.

'You remember, then.'

'It was in the middle of the village, at a cross roads, with no hot water and a terrific smell of dead crabs. And if you followed an arrow saying "Cinema" you could walk right out of the place, along a two-mile stretch of unadopted road and half-built houses, and the wind whipping in off the Atlantic like a whetted knife because there was nothing between you and Halifax, Nova Scotia – '

'And the sea, as far as the eye could make out in the mist and low cloud, staked out with long lines of straggling poles, that the damfool mussels climbed up and got scooped off by the local seafood industry – '

'Then you turned round and walked back, with your other cheek bulged with the gale this time, and found that the arrow saying "Cinema" was actually pointing to a sort of failed Methodist mission hall just across the road, screening John Mills speaking French with a stiff upper lip in a sunk submarine.'

'Yes,' I said. 'And back in the hotel they were laying the tables for an all-night fish harvest festival. Yes, indeed. Talk about total recall. Whoever it was must have painted a telling picture. The point is, who were they?'

'They were us,' he said.

'You're right. No wonder it's all coming back to me. It doesn't make any difference, though.'

'What to, for instance?'

'I've remembered now. It was Glad and Dai Morgan. Only they weren't telling us, we were telling them. It just shows how careful you'd have to be in a witness box. And Dai said, too true, look you – '

'He couldn't have been speaking Australian *and* Welsh.'

' – and he said they'd had just the same trouble somewhere else, and what they were looking for that year was the individual chalet-bungalow type holiday, with the rest of the world out of earshot.'

'It was like Dunkirk.'

'So they'd love Spotorno. What was?'

'Those mussel poles, winding out to sea in long, patient lines, waiting for the little ships.'

'It was the worst holiday we ever had,' I said.

He suddenly flared up at that, and told me not to make sweeping statements. What about Jersey, he said. And I could see we were in for an open-ended discussion so I asked him if he'd remembered the bread, which luckily he hadn't. There's nothing changes a subject like having to make a sudden U-turn in peak shopping traffic, and down to the station and round the roundabout and up to the car park opposite the baker's with its perky little Full board stuck out in front. Don't you find that?

Q. *It still doesn't seem quite clear from my notes whether it was you or Mr A who recommended Mr and Mrs Morgan to Spotorno?*

'No? (said Mrs A, arching her brows attractively). I thought I made that clear when he came in with the drinks. And incidentally, talking of changing subjects, we'd love to have you to lunch, if you don't mind butt-ends of old Camembert off paper picnic plates. We aren't right back in the domestic swing yet, I'm afraid. Or sometimes my husband fancies his hand at an omelette when we're fresh back from the omelette country, but I warn you it's a risk, and might have some bits of film in it.

Q. *I find it best not to leave things too long before running through one's notes, especially of this extremely rich and varied nature. Would you object, in the circumstances, if I made my own arrangements, resuming the investigation this afternoon?*

VII

'I called him brother, Englishman
and friend.'
William Wordsworth

———————————

Q. *An advertisement for a resort in Tenerife recently caught my eye, Mrs A,
with the punch line, 'A Great Place to Make Friends'. Could you say if this would
be an effective influence on your choice of a foreign holiday venue, or the state of the
marriage when you got there?*

I'M sorry you're off on a fresh tack (said Mrs A) because I woke in
the night with a feeling that I could have answered your yesterday's
question this morning, the one Mr A seems to have messed up, about
post-vacational recriminations, or PVR for short. He woke up, too,
actually, asking if it was Anglesey or Dubrovnik where he lost his
wallet. As a matter of fact, it was Cannes, so you can see you've
really got us going, and we had a touch of PVR over that, between
you and me, before we dozed off again. You don't think these probes
of yours do more matrimonial harm than good? Myself, I'm not at
all sure it's healthy, dwelling on the morbid past like this. The vital
thing, once you're unpacked, and you'll see we've made quite a bit
of progress this last day or two but don't sit on those binoculars,
hang them on the clock, the vital thing is to salvage the best and
forget the rest. Luckily, this is easier than you'd think, because the
other day we were telling Sam and Nancy Chatty about our X
holiday and it turned out they'd been there when the Hewitts were
there, and I clearly remember saying, 'You missed an absolute gem.
not going to Le Muy, didn't you realize you were only twenty miles
off?' This is what comes of learning the post-vacational disciplines
over the years, you see. If I'd spoken my mind to Mr A for letting
the Hewitts con him into X, when all three of them were exalted
with the Truepennys' mock posset – You were saying? Oh, well, as
long as it doesn't matter – I should have been bound to go widely
into chapter and verse, and the whole calendar of events would have
been carved on my heart, like Calais. Check this impulse, preferably

when it's at its strongest, and the wound will heal. All you'll remember, except under fresh surgery, as at the present time, is the happy hours, such as when one of the Leicester weft-minders, who'd been noticeably bossy throughout, got impatient with the waiter service, dished round the grated cheese at a table with eight mine-strones and it turned out to be coconut.

And again, of course, as far as the Chattys and the Hewitts went, it was a real stroke of luck that they hadn't been there when we were, a thing that puts X right up the charts whenever we discuss it now. What can you say really bad about a resort where the Chattys and the Hewitts could have been the first people you saw, and weren't?

Don't think I'm putting the boot in here, with Sam and Nancy. Not even with Tom and Tatty, drunken lapses apart. Surprise, surprise, I'm actually working round to the matter before the court, even though obliquely. If we're to get a rounded picture of social life in foreign parts, then any discussion on whether or not you want to make friends in Tenerife – or anywhere else for that matter, say North Rhine-Westphalia, why not – obviously can't overlook the friends you've got already. How many couples haven't we seen in our time, you and I, sauntering along the old Promenade des Anglais without a care in the world or a cloud in the sky, and suddenly they take off like four-minute milers up the nearest Avenue Marshal Foch, crying as they run, "My God, it's the Stephensons"? You've nothing against Stephensons, you understand. In fact he's just about the most respected dentist in your urban district, and she's continu-ally coming out top in the Housewives Guild flower arrangements. It's just that you don't take to the air at 40,000 feet for the fun of meeting them when you come down. You want the mind broadened, not nipped tight in a forceps or fixed in the bottom of a vase on a platform of weighted spikes. What you'd much prefer is a chat with a French dog in the cafe where you've sought asylum. You're not alone in this. If you risked a backward glance as you ran, you'd probably see the Stephensons legging it just as fast up the nearest Place of the Liberation.

If, that is, they're the decent, sensitive pair you always thought they were. There are those who aren't, and come galloping after you, though luckily they're the minority. They can be a particular menace if you've got a wasp sting in your foot, or similar disability. It's Mr A's stock objection when I start thumbing through the winter sports brochures. 'Fine thing,' he says – 'hobbling round Grenoble with your leg in a cast, and there are the Plimhorns, beaming and closing in.' It's a clever argument, you have to give him that, not to his face, of course, and on second thoughts we'd better have it stricken from the record, right?

No, it's a funny thing about friends, especially that minority. You can run into them in the interval at the Festival Hall, and they go off at the high squeal with plans to drop in on you next time they're running down to the coast, probably the weekend after next, only of course they can't be sure because it didn't occur to them they'd want their engagement books for the Dvorak cello concerto. Lovely, darlings such fun . . . and the next you see of them it's three years later at the National Film Theatre. 'But we must meet, darlings,' they say, and you say you can't wait, and in this way, possibly enriched by a card at Christmas, the association is kept up. But once foreign parts come into it the picture changes for the worse. It needs a crafty conjunction of circumstances, but that's not unheard of: viz., you run into them in the bar at the Old Vic, where they've ordered some exotic drink the barmaid's had to go out for, and during the delay that's going to make a hundred and fifteen people late for act two the topic of holidays comes up and it turns out you're going to be in the Dordogne, all four of you, during the identical fortnight. 'But, darlings – give give me something to write on, George – now exactly when are you booked in at Bergerac? But it's incredible, we're only forty miles up the river, we'll all dine together the very day you bowl up.' And naturally you don't expect to hear another word about it. Bad luck, though, in this case. The very day you bowl up, saddle sore, mud-caked, starving and stiff, there they are, you bet, George and Harriet Schwenk, been there for hours, all smiles and newly-pressed leisure wear and run off all the bath water.

I know you want the facts, so I have to admit that it's Mr A who lets us in. He's the one in the Old Vic bar who spills the dates and places like a man under truth-drugs, only breaking off to ask why I'm kicking him on the ankle. Left to me, I'd have us off the hook in no time, quick story about nothing settled but a vague plan for Iceland and even then it's all off if an aunt dies, and we're in the clear. As this is national frankness week, let me also admit that I don't know why he does this, except for a natural sweetness and simplicity of character which he'd be the first, I may say, to disclaim. It can hardly be Harriet and her type, because if her type's his type he made a fearful boob persuading me to accept this sapphire ring some

93

years back, a small stone but tasteful. Would I care to – ? No, if you don't mind, but I can't stop you asking at Somerset House, naturally.

No, my own diagnosis is that he has this very split personality about social relations abroad. He thinks before we go that he'll be able to rub along with just me and fifty million Frenchmen, or the nationals of our choice. But the time soon comes when it isn't enough, and even if the Schwenks walked in he'd probably . . . well, perhaps not the Schwenks, I want to be fair. But there it is, he gets this strange pining. Two days it's fine, keeps saying what a relief to hear a foreign language, because if they're talking a lot of twaddle you can't tell anyway, and he's managed to stop the headwaiter putting us at a table next to that old English berk with a Boothby bow-tie . . . The third day he begins to go broody, you can't get a word out of him except did you pack my book of Burmese proverbs, or something else he feels would make a link with home, and after dinner on the fourth night you see him coming back from the bar with a boyish grin and a big wrinkled old creature in a spotted bow.

'Darling,' he says, 'this is Mr – I never seem to get names, I'm sorry.'

'Nulke,' says the man, or as near as makes no difference.

'My wife. She doesn't always look like this, she's had her hair in the water, ha-ha. Darling, Mr Nulke's a retired research chemist from Harpenden, been telling me some very interesting stuff about pituitary secretions caused by feeding moles on rhubarb. He can't drink because of a liver condition, but he was asking at the bar for Murraymints, and they haven't any, and I knew you'd help him out.'

'Take two,' you say, which happens to be all you've got; you knew there was something you meant to get at the airport and now you know.

'Very kind,' he says, prodigally crunching. 'It's only a mild irritation in the cystic duct. My father had it all his life, was obliged to drink in the course of business, lived to be eighty and actually died of emphysema. I expect you've heard of the wineshippers, Nulke and Cretin, branches in London, Lisbon, Bordeaux, Mainz, Cadiz, Turin, Marseilles . . . '

After that, he joins you every night, never at a loss for some action-packed reminiscence about what Neville Chamberlain said to his uncle, or how his mother, formerly Lady Mary Bisto, was the toast of the Cotswolds and invented the first bone-free corset.

It's the herd instinct, wouldn't you say, in one of its tinier manifestations, and it's a funny thing about husbands, if they can herd with the wrong people they will. I don't know why this is, you only have to look at most Englishmen abroad to tell whether they're raving status-shooters or modest-stillness-and-humility men. If you can't tell, because they're stripped to the buff on the foreshore with no clue but a wet haircut, steer clear anyway, because all the odds are they belong to the first lot. In fact, it's when they defy identification in this way that you're most likely to get the voluntary blow-by-blow life story, with details of their tax-bracket, director's perks and influential friends, and perhaps – if that's the way it takes them – a quick family tree sketched in the sand with a nearby lobster claw.

Still, you can't always blame your husband in their case. The question of steering clear doesn't really come into it. The compulsive status man, once he's caught the faint waft of English voices, is along in no time presenting himself in the shadow of your umbrella.

'I'm wondering if you could oblige me with a light?' he says, splashing from his held-in chest on to your spread-out newspaper. And your lawful wedded idiot, instead of saying, 'Drop dead', with a sporting chance of nipping the thing in the bud, springs up for his smoker's survival kit, kicking your bikini full of grit.

'I see you've got a Gimcrack,' says this creep, handing the lighter back. 'Mine's one of the new Superglyms, present from their Chairman, as a matter of fact. Lord Boggs, I expect you know him. But it happens to be solid gold with an emerald flintscrew, and my wife makes me keep it in the hotel safe. By the way, I'm Nigel Trott-Vasasour, Anglo-American Rubbish Recovery – no, no, try one of these, I get them specially made for me in Mozambique.'

'This is my wife. We're – '

'I'm only here for a couple of days, got to get on to Spain, Italy, back through Israel for a look at the new separator plant, then Germany – '

'Our names – '

' – and then London for Covent Garden on the seventeenth, got two daughters in the Royal Ballet. Strange thing, heredity, because the boys are both on the science side. Torquil's a big wheel with the Massachusetts Institute of Technology, and Dominic runs the entire technical side of Transglobal Resins.'

'We – '

'Goodbye. Fun meeting you.'

And he can say that again. You can see by the way he flops out on his own bit of beach and lets his chest go that he's a happy, relaxed man, a weight off his mind. No danger now that the subtopian-looking duo at the next umbrella will write him off as a struggling haberdasher or failed speech therapist.

Not that they have to have a gold lighter in the safe to get an urge to justify themselves like this. It's simply a matter of establishing any kind of ascendancy, and picking a field where they can be pretty sure of doing it. We've had men stop us on the way to the beach-showers before now, just to list their kids' A-Levels, or tell us that when they were in Ibiza last year they stayed at the same hotel as Princess Alexandra's ex-nanny. And on the whole they don't make up a pack of lies, I'll give them that. You can tell this when they send the waiter over from their table with a note saying, 'What about a drink afterwards? Horace Lee, BA, Deputy Sales Director, East Midlands Gas Board'. Anyone working up a holiday fantasy life could improve on that.

Our friends the Wauchops were badly caught like this a couple of years ago at Spezia. I needn't say that it was Cyril, not Irma, who took up with this millionaire playboy-cum-ex-racing-driver who kept an Alfa-Romeo, a Bentley and three Ferraris at his castle in Bedfordshire, with forty rooms, four lifts, two swimming pools and a wife running the biggest matrimonial agency in London but qualifying as absent friends at the moment because she was doing the round of her New York, Boston and Philadelphia branches. So he said.

'If you ask me,' said Irma, after he'd loosed off all this stuff at them out at sea, happening to be on an adjacent pedalo, 'he's just a poor little psychopathic lost property superintendent – in some quite superior position, possibly, like the Tate Gallery or somewhere, but he has these dreams. I didn't by chance hear you accepting an invitation to drop in on him for lunch when we get home?'

'It's hard to say no,' Cyril said.

'Well, you can say no now,' said Irma. 'And then keep dodging, before he touches you for ten francs for the fruit-machines, loses the lot and shoots himself with a borrowed gun.'

They hadn't been married long, or she would have known that this was no line to take. If she'd left him to mull for a day or two he'd have come up with the lost property theory on his own account, as likely as not. Or her even better course would have been to say, 'Oh, marvellous, I've never been in a castle socially, only I haven't a thing to wear. I'll tell you what, we could drop off at Harrods the moment we're back, I've got to have a coat for the autumn, anyway, and I might just as well . . . '

But there, you can always see the right thing to do after you've done the wrong one. The whole holiday was dominated by debates about this man. Irma said if he was rolling in the stuff why were his collars frayed, and Cyril said if you're rolling in the stuff you can walk around with your front zip dangling and no comments.

'But he goes by bus everywhere.'

'Wouldn't you, if you were stuck the rest of the year driving a stable full of racing cars? Besides, he can't go by bus at home without losing face. Here it's a nice relax for him.'

'Lives in a castle, my foot,' said Irma.

'Why shouldn't he?'

'Corfe Castle is my guess, dossing in the ruins.'

'Now, steady,' said Cyril. 'How would you like it if he was spreading it around that I'm not the design superintendent for Wessex Consolidated Mattresses? Anyway, we can prove it. He's invited — '

'You prove it, leave me out of it.'

'I'll do that.'

'Do that.'

'Fine.'

'And if his wife's there, and not fixing marriages on the Boston, New York, Philadelphia run, ask her for a couple of basic leaflets on mutual respect for an opposing opinion.'

'One, I'll ask her for. For you. I flatter myself I don't need one.'

That's the trouble with holidays. Bags of time for the big fight. At home you can usually bank on the phone going before the end of the first round. Saved by the bell, they call that. But Irma and Cyril were still exchanging punishment while they waited for the bags to come up at Heathrow. She was well in the lead on points by then, and finally, in the coach back to the BEA terminal, she practically had him on the canvas. 'Go and see then, mule-head,' she said. 'But when it turns out a load of old cobblers, be man enough to say so. Don't come home with a lot of imaginary champagne and butlers and lapis-lazuli all bathrooms. Just admit I was right all along and we'll forget the whole thing.'

And talking of being honest (said Mrs A, faltering uncharacteristically and biting her lower lip for a moment), it's rather . . . I don't quite know . . . it isn't easy to . . .

Q. Yes, Mrs A?
A. I wish I'd never started this story.
Q. Are you feeling quite well?
A. No.
Q. We sometimes allow a short adjournment for witnesses to compose themselves. Would you care — ?

Cyril Wauchop (resumed Mrs A, rallying) went. Not specially, just happened to be in Bedfordshire spreading the word for Consolidated Mattresses, saw this castle signposted, made an impulse detour . . .

Q. Yes, Mrs A?
A. You do know that I'm all for women hanging together and not showing one another up in a bad light? I'd like your assurance.
Q. You have it. What happened?

What happened was that the millionaire lost property man was floating around in one of his swimming pools. Absolutely delighted to see Cyril, rang the butler on his poolside telephone to bring out some champagne and foie gras sandwiches, then a short tour of the Ferraris, Bentley, Alfa and an E-type Jag he'd forgotten to mention. Cyril told Mr A afterwards that missing out the E-type was the only point where the original prospectus could be faulted. Well, he didn't see the wife, he admitted that. And he wasn't there long enough to check the bathrooms, either, because his host was leaving for the airport in half an hour, meeting her from a business trip to Philadelphia, Boston and New York. Showed Cyril the week's Western Union cables, sending her love and asking after the horses. The only bright spot that came out of the whole diabolical episode was that he naturally couldn't tell Irma.

Q. She wouldn't have believed him?

No doubt he'd take that into consideration. More important, it was a triumph for the science of husband-conditioning. Just shows how you can train up even Cyril type material over quite a short period. He told Mr A that he came to his decision on the drive home, with practically no heart-searching at all. Put the car away, walked in, kissed her, admired her new rinse, held forth a bit about a shop in Bedford where they'd got a smashing display of Consolidated

Mattresses – and never told her about the castle at all. Only two years married, and he'd already learnt that for a man with his sights set on the patter of little feet and beyond, the old 'I told you so', even at its most well-earned, is a surefire gateway to the empty nursery.

But human wives everywhere get terribly torn in their allegiances at times. The maddening thing for me (said Mrs A, her restored composure pierced with a sudden metallic glint) is that I wonder how long I can go without telling her.

Q. For her own good?
A. For mine. How would you feel about some strong black coffee?

VIII

'Missing so much and so much'
Frances Cornford

Q. *A small point, Mrs A, going through my notes last night. They seem to abandon your recently completed motoring holiday with great abruptness. As it was only last Monday that you returned, and I quote, h'm, from 'slurping up the kilometres' I should have thought it would have been fresh in your mind. So why all the hearsay evidence concerning persons not before this court, the Weemses, the Harringtons, the Garforth-Smythes and the luckless Gerald and Mopsy Queenbridge, to name but a few?*

HORTENSE HALFHIDE (said Mrs A, speaking rapidly and on a higher note than usual) used to plan their holidays until her eyes dropped out, and even then they often got back without a smell of their major objectives. Her husband, Pulteney, told Mr A that she started on next year's in the plane coming back from this. Or should I say this's, but I suppose you'll go through all this for grammar before sending it to the printers, or whatever you think of doing with it. Don't bother hunting for the Halfhides in your notebook because I haven't told you about them yet. And if you're trying to ask whether they're real names I can only say that if Bulwer Lytton couldn't think up any more likely heroes than Eugene Aram and Ernest Maltravers, let alone Kenelm Chillingly, you'd hardly expect me to come up with Hortense and Pulteney Halfhide out of my head. He happens to be a very well-breeched electro-plater and you'll find him in the yellow pages for the Eastbourne area. It was over their 1967 holiday that he finally left Hortense, which in fact wasn't –

Q. *Mrs. A.*

– her fault at all. He'd had much better excuses in other years, when she booked for the Baalbek festival the fortnight after it closed, for instance, or the informal one-class cruise where Pulteney only packed his ratting trousers and found everyone else changing for

dinner. And after all that, it had to be this whirlwind tour of the
Holy Land that finally blew up the union. She'd been working on it
for three hundred and fifty-nine days, and it was only for six, all
marked off in one-hour stints on graph paper, Jaffa and Haifa,
Hermon and Hebron, Tyre and Sidon, Sodom and –
Q. Mrs. A!
It coincided to the minute with the Arab-Israeli war, or it would
have done if the pilot hadn't picked up the Keep Out signal on his
glide-path into Lydda, just touched the runway and bounced right
back to Gatwick, where they had this terrible scene, with Pulteney
all for getting back to Bishop's Stortford to paint the larder, and
Hortense already working on a week in the Hereward the Wake
country. It may sound like an extreme case, but it's nothing to –
Q. Order!
– the case of Petunia and Pirbright Wainscot. She was a Miss
Woodpecker, luckily, so all her initialled handkerchiefs –

Q. *These proceedings are suspended for one minute by the court's watch, during
which the witness will try to compose herself. Is that clear?*

*   *   *

Q. *Thank you. Slurping up the kilometres, Mrs A?*

Slurping was piling it on (said Mrs A, somewhat calmed by lipstick but still avoiding the court's eye). Sipping would be more like
it. Incidentally, you'd think to hear Mr A talk that it's me who hangs
around the sherry parties, seducing barrel-chested executives into
working us a pass into an Elastic Stockings convention at Clermont-
Ferrand – and I'm not joking: whole schedules have been ditched
before now, rather than waste the free tickets to a bicycle museum.
His proud stroke this year looked a bit more practical on the surface, I have to admit. Half-price car hire, it was, from a top string-
puller with the French tourist people in London. He was Mr A's
new name-drop for weeks, and the name was only Simpson anyway.
Funny, that, being on the pay-roll of the Quai d'Orsay and as English
a nit as you could want to meet: still, you do get that: go into the
Piccadilly branch of the Bank of Pernambuco and they're no more
Pernambucan than Norman St John-Stevas.
This French Simpson also produced a crisp-looking To Whom It
May Concern, or Attestation, as they call them over there, and Mr A

was in a very excited state about it. He just laughed when I warned him they'd closed the Lascaux Caves because tourists' breath was melting the drawings: show them the Attestation, he said, and they'd have them open like a Sesame. I never saw what it was in there, because he kept it clamped to his chest like a plaster. Couldn't read a word of it, mind you, except his own name, but he said there was a list of powerful contacts on the back, all eager to grab us with their trunks and drop us in the best seats at any circus we fancied.

They have this quality of innocence, you know? Like a two-year-old baby seen from the back, with that frail little eggshell bonce and its ears sticking out, not a clue how hard life's going to hit it.

We had a good flight over. An engine coughed once, and I saw him unfolding his document to show the pilot and get us priority down the escape chute, but in fact he didn't need it for another half hour or so, when he spotted the car delivery man at the airport.

'Bonjour, bonjour, bonjour,' he breezed. 'Just lisez this, and let's have the ignition key.' He likes to do the opening bit of fluency, then I have to take over.

The man read it right to the end and handed it back with a snigger.

'Nine hundred francs deposit,' he said.

Of course, you can only theorize. France has this self-assurance nowadays, stands on its own feet, going it alone and so forth. Not like a dozen years back, when you could hardly step ashore at Dieppe without being asked to form a government, so it's possible foreigners don't cut the ice they did. Or there's another theory, which I only have Mr A's word for. Apparently there's a class of men, thwarted raconteurs who want to be the life of the party but can't remember stories, and they carry bits of rude typewriting to hand round the bar and raise a laugh that way. Perhaps the car hire man thought he'd got one of these, and somehow missed the joke – this can happen in such circles, I'm told, and all they can manage is the snigger.

'What's he on about?' said Mr A.

'Nine hundred francs deposit,' I said.

'Etes-vous – ?' said Mr A. 'What's the French for are you out of your mind?'

It was a setback. You expect setbacks, but at the least you can usually get off the airport first. I needn't tell you, with your grasp of the international currency position, that when you've planned a safari deep into the truffle country, expecting your transport at cut rates and paid for in sterling when you get back anyway, one of those legally legal but morally damaging recourses that honest citizens are manoeuvred into by repressive administrations – I'm sorry, the turbot came wrapped in a *Times* leader page yesterday, and I was reading a bit off its soft underbelly in the kitchen mirror – in a case like this, what I'm saying, you don't want to see more than half your foreign capital creamed off in the first minute, leaving you five nights' lodging, eating on alternate days, and then over to begging in the streets.

'You'll have to ring London,' said Mr A, to the man. 'Sonnez Londres.'

'Nine hundred francs,' said the man. 'Deposit.'

'You can't expect him to pronounce a difficult name like Simpson,' I said. 'Why don't you ring him?'

'If you think,' said Mr A, 'we're going to have money to fling down the long-distance French telephone service – '

'He'll have to ring Nantes, then,' I said, which was apparently his branch office. It took some getting across, and he didn't like it, but in the end he went off inside.

We'd had two strokes of luck, actually, hardly noticed them at the time. One was that all the funds were in travellers' cheques, and the car man wanted no part of them. I think they were a new thing to him, he'd reacted like a Sioux chief with his first bit of looking glass. The other was the backward state of the airport, a joint so short of amenities that it would have thought a bureau de change was a convertible writing desk. And now we had the third stroke, at any rate in Mr A's view.

'Look,' he said, swinging the ignition key from his thumb. The man, no doubt thrown into disarray by missing the joke in the Attestation, had handed the key back with it.

'Get in, we're off,' said Mr A, pressing the cigar lighter, winker knob, wiper button headlamp switch and starter.

The man reappeared, shouting something.

'What does he say?' said Mr A, as we reversed into a mesh fence and catapulted into the forward gears.

No one knows what a burden lies on an interpreter's shoulders. It was a split-second decision I had to make.

'He says nothing to pay.'

'I told you we could rely on old Simpson,' he said. 'Which way for the truffle country?'

You like to see them happy, that's the trouble. You don't knock a baby's plastic Sooty out of its hands to tell it about income tax and race riots. But it means repressions, of course. My instinct was to suggest picking up a couple of false number plates somewhere, because they'd have the road blocks out any minute now. Taking and driving away, I wanted to tell him, wouldn't just mean one of those amusing roadside courts, with a twenty-franc fine and an admonition from the rustic bench; it'd be separate dungeons in the Château d'If, and not half Monte Cristo's luck with the break out, just the weary passage of time, and the very occasional question asked about us in the House.

It took some doing, but for six miles I didn't utter, and it was too late then, because we hit the road block. We were well back in the jam, but up front I could see the peaked hats passing from driving window to driving window, waving the innocent through. Even then it seemed best to let the uniformed branch break the bad news to him. They're used to it, after all. I'll go and make some coffee.

Q. *I beg your pardon?*
A. *I'll go and make some coffee.*
Q. *Yes, I know. But what happened about —?*
A. *Being Saturday, I'd better heave the grocery cartons off the back step and unpack them. I can't expect him to —*
Q. *Mrs A. What about the road block?*
A. *— break off cleaning the car in its final stages, doing the tar specks with eucalyptus. Black or white?*
Q. *Could it, in the circumstances, be extremely black?*
A. *Me, too. You ought to take a turn round the house, you look as if you could do with a breath of fresh air.*

*   *   *

I can't say I've noticed that she's been acting peculiarly, no (said Mr A, straightening up from buffing an exhaust pipe). She gave a bit of a groan when I sat in the back seat just now, but of course her suspension sub-frame hasn't been under load for nearly three weeks, and probably after she's done a mile or two she'll get over it. Besides, I'd rather have a groan than a squeak any time. That little French heap I've just been driving — What? Oh, sorry, talking about Mrs A, are you? Yes, well, I don't know whether I'd call it acting peculiarly, exactly, but I know what you mean. Beneath their gay exterior they're often subject to hidden strains, leading to apparently random outbursts of wild talk, or sudden decisions to restuff cushions. Any evidence on recent events might be hard for her to recollect in tranquillity. You never know how these things will take them. Breaking off in the middle of a story like that could be what the psychiatrists call approach rejection. Something very similar happens with carburettors, when the breather pipe from the rocker box brings up too much oil, and the filter-leaves –

Q. *What happened about the road block? Please. This would be about six miles from the airport, I see from my notes.*

I don't know about any road block. She probably meant the ferry. That would be about six miles, but nothing happened, as far as I remember. Paid the peaked hats at the gangway, rolled aboard, and we were crossing the Loire estuary at a breathtaking two knots, all set for the truffle country. Not that we ever got there, but still. I shouldn't risk that garden chair. Let me open the lid and you can perch in the boot. I often do that.

On second thoughts, though, something slightly odd did happen a few miles further on. She'd been quiet for an unusually long time, for her, and then she suddenly burst out at me about tomatoes. Tomatoes, yes. You hear aright. She said I'd promised last year not to plant any more, and this year I'd done it again, and did I realize she'd been breaking her arms night and morning watering the damned things ever since, just so that they could ripen while we were away and be rotten when we got back. So naturally I diagnosed a hidden strain, entirely unrelated to tomato-breeding, of course, but in a small hot car far from home they have to blow any gasket that comes to hand. I quite understood that. The trick would be finding out what these tomatoes were sublimating. The general area was probably monetary, following our encounter with the Idiot of Nantes. Pin-pointing it might be rather more delicate.

And between you and me, I was feeling a twinge of anxiety in the monetary area myself. I put on a brave profile for the passenger seat, but I couldn't help thinking that a sum of nine hundred francs doesn't float into a dim French skull from pure invention. Even the shout of nothing to pay didn't entirely sweep the figure under the carpet. It was there in the books, if you asked me, and somebody, some time, was going to want it. I also felt a growing insecurity over the man Simpson. I wasn't too keen to bring this into the open either. For one thing, you like to see them happy; for another, you don't hand them ammunition on a plate, and she'd already shown a touch of scepticism – without even knowing that I'd only met him at a French exhibition of dog's bedding in the Whitechapel art gallery. She'd still gone on about him to some purpose. Said she was under the impression that I'd taken the pledge on all types of Gallup ever since the affair of Beefy, the boat train, Mr Bishop and the pickle factory – I think if you turn up the court's earlier records you'll find . . . Oh, you do? Good.

It wasn't an easy charge to answer. The truth is, as someone may have pointed out, that hope springs eternal in the human breast, and it's only human to hope for a Gallup nearer to your heart's desire one of these days. Like going back to a pair of shoes that crippled you six months ago, on the off chance that your feet have shrunk since then. I scorned this line of defence, even with a wife who tries the shoe trick all the time, often extends it to foundation garments, and once even to an old wrist watch, in case it had collected enough dust after three years in the sideboard to cure it of gaining five minutes in ten. Yes, indeed. One thing you learn in a marriage is to reject even the juiciest debating points.

Could this Simpson prove a broken reed? Over a couple of free gins in a Dog Society's hospitality room you don't really find out what sort of reed a man is. I left before he did, and if he stayed the distance with the hospitality he could easily have confused me with someone called Schmückbohm, who wanted to be met with a chauffeur-driven limousine off a night flight at Fuhlsbuttel. It's true that he'd come up with the Attestation, but he'd fixed this on the phone there and then, leaving the booth door open so that I could admire his crisp authority with the miniskirt at the far end. It certainly told the world that I was de haut standing, and that Simpson serait vivement reconnaissant à toutes autorités compétentes de bien vouloir aider me, but that was just him talking. If the competent authorities weren't interested where were you? It hadn't gone a bomb so far on the hired car side. What did the future hold, when we squeaked to a halt in two weeks' time, packed to the larynx with truffles, and found a posse of executives from Nantes barring the tarmac with linked arms and demanding nine hundred alien nicker, plus mileage and dilapidations . . . and our best offer a couple of groats with holes in the middle and half a pot of roebuck pâté?

And there was another thing. Even if we weren't foiled by the Schmückbohm-Fuhlsbuttel effect, and no basic cock-up – sorry, mishandling – had occurred, I suddenly realized I was somewhat hazy on another vital particular. Was the half-price lark just for the hire, which wouldn't save more than a few goes of moules marinières? Or did it run to the mileage on the clock? Because that's where your outgoings really roar up into the astronomy. I eased up on the accelerator, damping the flow of gold.

'Why are we stopping?' It was her first word since the tomatoes.

'While we're here,' I said, returning from a nearby glade, 'let's just do a quick sum on how the money's going to hold out.'

From the answers we got, as always with connubial mathematics, we could have been working on different problems. Nothing new there, and I wouldn't have worried . . . but the difference between hers and mine was nine hundred and eighty francs. Forget the eighty. The data was rough. It was the nine hundred that went through me like a blunt bodkin. She'd calculated on being nine hundred down the drain to start with. It could only mean she knew something.

What, I asked myself, had the man really shouted? It was a moment of high suspense . . . I think I shall go indoors now, it's getting a bit too cloudy for her to look her best. She needs the sun.

Q. *I'm afraid I'm not – what was that?*
A. *Otherwise you lose the effect of the two-tone.*
Q. *Mr A. Please. You surely don't intend to leave me – ?*
A. *No, no, no. You come inside too. There's probably some coffee in there now.*

I'm not ashamed to state (said Mr A, absently wiping his neck with a wash-leather) that in this unromantic French lay-by – it's no sugar for you, isn't it? – carpeted with empty Gitanes packets and old corks, flanked by piles of road-grit, and in the shadow of a split notice board with amateur lettering forbidding us to hunt, an act of true love was played out.

Q. *H'm.*
Too hot for you? Oh, good. A strangely touching situation, found only in the best marriages, if that doesn't sound too arrogant. Each spouse keeping a secret fear unspoken to preserve the other's peace of mind. Very wonderful, really. You can get it sometimes when you both spot separately that the TV's on the blink, but let concealment, like a what-is-it –

That's it. Feed on your damask cheek, if you like to put it like that. It was a time for great gentleness.

'Is there something,' I said to her, with great gentleness, 'that you want to tell me?'

'So you've found it,' she said.

'Found what?'

'A tiny knitted garment, tucked down the back of the sofa.'

'You needn't be so flaming funny,' I said, great gentleness only having a limited staying power with me. 'What did he shout?'

'Who shout?'

'Damn it, the nan from Mantes, the man from Nantes. Did he shout nothing to pay, or did he not shout it?'

'All right, then,' she said. 'I wasn't going to tell you, to preserve your peace of mind. He not shouted it, and I hope you're satisfied. As far as I could tell over your gear-crashing all he shouted was No Reply.'

'Yes, well,' I said. 'To preserve yours, I wasn't going to tell you that Simpson, in all likelihood, is a broken reed.'

'Right,' she said. Quite calm. In a real crisis they come through like queens. She could have stormed off about the mouse-nest under the airing cupboard, or needing a new hall carpet because when you wheeled the trolley into the curled-up edge the Worcester sauce fell over and broke a cup. All she said was, 'How far can we get on what's in the tank?'

'Nowhere near a truffle,' I said.

'Let's go,' she said.

We put the nine hundred francs in a sealed envelope and tried to forget it. Not easy, really, because every time we sat together over a wineless repast in some no-star dosshouse wishing we could afford another small omelette it was the sealed envelope that came to mind. We walked a good deal. Even the French don't charge you much for that. We thought about the addresses on the back of the Attestation, all well out of petrol radius and walking distance, except for a dignitary in Poitiers said to be the king-pin of the whole French tourist complex for the region of Poitou-Charentes. I regarded him as my ace in the hole. If we kept up the starvation we might be able to limp to Poitiers as a last resort. It would be the last, all right, because according to present calculations, which were now getting very fine, we should roll in there with a bone-dry tank, and nothing but a well-pulled string would roll us out again.

The Attestation hadn't exactly proved itself so far. I tried it on the barman of a transport cafe where the mustard had a skin on it, but he didn't even snigger, just whipped away the whole cruet and went off duty. Mrs A tried to keep my spirits up by saying that if it worked at all it would be in the higher echelons. Flourish it in the Elysée Palace, with a bit of table-banging, and you'd get a kiss on both cheeks from Couve de Murville; but show it to a street trader in Paimboeuf, asking to be directed to the cheapest bed in town, and it was right over his head.

One thing, we saw places this holiday to give us the edge over the Fiskes of this world for all time. It's hard to remember the names now, that's the only difficulty, quaint little primitive settlements, hostile to strangers, mostly uncharted, and with terrible drains. I remember Paimboeuf, because it's just like the French to hit on an ear-tickler like Breadbeef and then muck it up in the spelling. I forget where it was that the landlord told the rest of the bar, according to my interpreter, that we were only in there out of the rain. It wasn't our fault we'd had to order one sandwich and two plates. Then there was the one with only five houses, grouped round a square full of farm machinery apparently dropped by helicopter –

'That was where,' said Mrs A, admitting a whiff of mayonnaise through the serving hatch, 'they thought we were stealing their dog.'

'If I've told her once not to talk to strange dogs – '

'How was I to know it was sacred? The whole village came out – '

'Over eight people.'

' – grabbed the dog and rushed back indoors.'

'Cursing us in old French,' said Mr A, 'and crossing themselves.'

'It was called something like Malvenue-la-Bastide,' said Mrs A, 'and we were in such a panic to make good our escape that we ran over the Thermos.'

'You're thinking of the place near Angers, after we'd hawked the flask up and down all three streets, begging a fill of coffee, but for money, and nobody – '

'Anyway,' said Mrs A, who could now be heard slicing cucumber, 'at least we all know what happened in Angers.'

'We do indeed.'

'Do we not.'

'And how.'

'It wasn't established how,' said Mrs A. 'You were driving. I think you'd better give your statement on that, and then ask the court if it fancies an adjournment for this bit of salmon.'

Q. *What happened in Angers, Mr A?*

We opened the sealed envelope, that's what (said Mr A), owing to being rammed up the rear by a large white Peugeot in the evening rush hour. I take full responsibility. I made the mistake of braking rather than maim a flock of pedestrians. This isn't French practice, and the man in the Peugeot was well within his rights to keep going, everyone agreed on that, bystanders, gendarmes, a huissier de justice, the man in the Peugeot and even the pedestrians. Naturally, when your feux have to be remplaced, and your échappement has to be remised en état – I quote the details from the repair bill for two hundred and twenty four francs – you have to stay at any handy five-star whose back yard you can crawl into pending the morrow and another day of garage opening. Even if it means raiding your sealed envelope and wishing you had a couple more just like it.

Mrs A won't mind my saying, I think, that these events caused a degree of nervous hyper-excitation on her part. She didn't feel up to the interpreting at the garage next morning, but she had the decency to watch me from the balcony of our room as I manoeuvred the car, now with an added flat tyre, a delayed reaction, through a herd of horses that were being shod out there by a mobile blacksmith. I often think we don't know our resources of courage and grit until we're called on to show them, and I was a proud man as I returned the two miles on foot to report that I'd beaten the garage down from thirty-six hours to twenty-four.

'How much?' she said.

'Thirty-six to twenty-four,' I said.

'Money, you dope!'

They aren't always easy to please. I hadn't risked the French for money. When it comes to languages I thrive on small triumphs. A man who clanks into a repair-shop, points to his splintered backside, explains that his auto is blessée, and gets understood immediately, doesn't want to take a further plunge and ruin the effect.

It was decided, all the same, to proceed to Poitiers with no more than twenty-four hours' delay. Simpson's time of testing was at hand. And I'm going to surprise the court here.

Q. *Not for the first time, may I say?*

He came through with flying colours, did Simpson, and if that isn't a surprise I don't know what is. I admit to a shade of disappointment over the king-pin of the whole French tourist complex for the region of Poitou-Charentes, however, who hadn't a syllable of English to his nom. I suppose it's something we second-class powers have to get used to, but it makes you realize what it's been like for the Serbs all these years. So it was good going, although I say it, to convince him that I wasn't selling anything, in trouble with the Customs, or arranging for a party of ninety to follow an old pilgrim route from Aix-la-Chapelle to St James of Compostela on motor-bikes. Better going still, getting him to stick the French treasury with a longish call to London, via Paris: and best of all, perhaps, passing the half-hour delay gazing across his desk at him in dumb-show small talk, without cracking and running. Even he felt the strain once or twice, suddenly went into a back room and loaded me with coloured brochures entitled Visitez la Cité d 'Angers. Which I'd done, of course.

The first surprise about Simpson was that he was there, and not away for six months on a Canadian lecture tour. Second, he remembered me. Third, he said he didn't understand what I was worrying about. Bung the car in the airport, leave the key in the bar and come home. Couldn't be anything simpler than that, he said, could there? I had to cede the point. He laughed a lot over the Peugeot incident, in fact that's what took up most of the call time. And then he said, oh, by the way if I was in London on Tuesday week –

'Which you will be,' said Mrs A, to the faint scent of salmon.

– and cared to be at an exhibition of French bottling machinery, with wine-tasting –

'Which you won't be,' said Mrs A.

'But –'

'Not if Simpson's going to be,' said Mrs A. 'It's ready.' She closed the hatch.

Hidden strains (said Mr A). Random outbursts of wild talk. What's she sublimating now? Can't be Simpson.

I admit we had our uneasy moments, and you could take the view that it was his fault, in an indirect sort of way. Of course, we didn't get any truffles. On the other hand, if it hadn't been for him, we shouldn't have come home with the best part of four hundred and fifty francs. Come on, if you don't mind eating in the kitchen.

IX

'I met a traveller from an antique
land.'
Percy Bysshe Shelley

Q. *Reverting to the herd instinct in husbands, Mrs A, do I take it that, in the interests of the marriage, they should resist this in all its forms? What are your views on fraternizing with the indigenous populations, for instance?*

IN the interests of the marriage (replied Mrs A) they should avoid herding with the sort of herd they always pick to herd with, for some reason. It's this that lumbers a wife with the Nulkes of this world, for coffee and brandies every evening for a fortnight and fourteen instalments of a serial about their chlorestorol content and why they can't wear tight suspenders. As to fraternizing with the – how did you put that?

Q. *Indigenous populations*

It's good. As to fraternizing with the locals, I'm all for it. Selectively and in moderation, of course. I take the view that a week in Wittenberg without exchanging so much as a word with a Wittenberger, and probably missing Luther's tomb as a result, might just as well be spent in Worksop, Notts. No Wittenberger in Worksop, believe me, wastes a moment before sounding off with, 'Good morning, afternoon, evening, I am cold, warm, frozen, when is the next omnibus for Sherwood Forest, Sheffield, the Dukeries?' The trouble with the British male tourist and husband, of whom we could take Mr A as a handy example, is that he has this deep-seated suspicion complex. Even after a mere twenty minutes from Lydd to Le Touquet be braces himself for a land of twisters, layabouts, ponces and pimps, whereas the British female wife simply sees them as colourful and different. This is all the odder, really, when you remember she's been warned from the cradle that she only has to step ashore at Dieppe and it's a sack over her head and first stop Haroun-Al-Raschid Street, Bagdad.

I was temped to exult somewhat when Mr A lost his wallet in Cannes a few years ago, an incident that still troubles his dreams occasionally, as it did the other night. We'd come in by one of those French bus companies that sound like an international pact, Sati, Seato, Nato, Sita, it doesn't matter. Or are they the Italian ones? It's not the way to come into Cannes, as a matter of fact, and it gave Mr A an even deeper sense of inferiority and mistrust. I'd warned him it was the film festival that week, so you can bet he took it the other way and said it would be just the week to go. But after climbing out of the bus with a load of old hold-alls and rolled-up raincoats – they'd had a lot of thunderstorms that summer, though on this particular day, I remember, the sun blazed throughout from a cloudless sky, as advertised – on to a Croisette where the Cadillac convertibles cruised in mass formation like May Day in Moscow, except that they'd mostly got the Richard Burtons in the back, he soon began wearing his whipped look.

He cheered up a bit when he thought he saw Ursula Andress on the beach with about a hundred and sixteen photographers, but it didn't last. Moving in smartly to get a better look, he rammed his toe on the iron stanchion of a crush barrier designed to prevent any such intrusion into privacy. I'd warned him against sandals, but he wouldn't have it, and it served him right. Not that I wasn't sympathetic, particularly as he dropped his raincoat on recoil and had it run over by Rex Harrison's Rolls-Royce. And it was obviously necessary to take the weight off his foot at a convenient cafe, which I needn't tell you are in plentiful supply around there, for any-one with fifteen bob to blow on a small, weak drink.

But he was in a fidgety state, what with his toe and Ursula Andress. Couldn't pick a table to suit him. If they hadn't got rocky legs they had obvious French con men sitting at them, or they were dead in the line of some menacing old scruff touting lottery tickets, or placed so that every time the sun-blind flapped it put one of his arms in the shade. So he'd thrown his palm beach jacket – more alpaca, actually, but leave them their illusions – over about six little white wrought-iron chair backs before he really took to one. And we were still working out what we could order, and leave the return bus fare intact, when he suddenly clutched up all the gear and was leading the way to the cafe adjoining. Masterful, really.

'Now what?' I said.

'You must have seen. Some French fink was coming round to all the tables in there, trying to shake down the clientele. Think he had a display folder of dirty postcards. My God, what a country.'

It gave him something to go on about all through the small, weak drinks, and it was very therapeutic, I think. Then he found his wallet was missing and had his relapse. Blasted sneak-thieves, he said. Now what did we do? Passports gone. Traveller's cheques. Receipt for last week at the hotel, and when they came to charge us again, as a matter of routine, not a stitch of evidence to prove we'd paid already.

I forget what I said for comfort. Some small pensée from my vade-mecum of soft words for all occasions. Anyway, I wasn't half-way through it when he went pale beneath his tan and pointed a trembling finger. The dirty-postcard man, having cleaned up at the neighbour establishment, was weaving craftily over.

'Monsieur?' he said, proffering his wares.

'Sh,' I said to Mr A, well before cue.

'Get lost!' yelled Mr A.

The man was delighted. 'Lost, yes!' he said, and handed over the wallet. He was the proprietor from next door. One of his waiters had found it on a chair and turned it in.

You'd think, wouldn't you, after an experience of this kind, that he'd soft-pedal on those remarks about wog skindivers with chests like burnt lawns, which I fancy you may have got down under a recent date? But their prejudices run terribly deep, of course, and you can't wonder the United Nations haven't got far with uniting the nations. I know just who he had in mind when he said that, incidentally – a very well set-up chartered accountant. It's true his remark wasn't a hundred per cent race prejudice. It was partly because he's a bit short, personally, on aqua-lung talent and torso shrubbery . . . not that I don't prefer the plain design myself, in case you misunderstand me at all. But none of that would have mattered if this had been an English chartered accountant, instead of a Greek one. Just happened to surface on a bit of the Aegean shore where we were taking a little iced retzina and goat's milk cheese, and quite spontaneously begged my acceptance of this freshly speared red mullet. Nothing wrong in that. I'd like to know how often anything of the sort occurs at Bridlington or Lytham St Annes. No, it was being a Greek that put him beyond the pale; even in Greece, where, as I pointed out at the time, while he was arranging with a shack up the beach to fry the mullet for us, he had a good deal more right to be than we had. It was when he came back with the sizzling pan, and turned out to have such fluent English that he could discuss wheel-balancing and automatic transmission, that Mr A softened a bit and shot the strip of movie referred to recently in his incompetent, irrelevant and immaterial evidence. It was mostly close-ups of the fish, but at least it suggested a shy twitch of the hand of friendship. Unfortunately, the chartered accountant had to pack up his harpoon, put a shirt on and get back to Tripolis next day to carry on his chartered accounting. I was very upset about this. I'm sorry? No, no – not off the record at all, but thanks for thinking of it. I was only upset – chiefly upset, let's say – because I should have liked the association to blossom. This man might have proved to be Mr A's shining key to Europe, a very decent feller in spite of being a wog, could have turned out to be keen on cricket, or quoted Winston Churchill or something, might have broken down a few prejudices for good.

We lost him too soon, that was the trouble, and next summer in Italy, by a bit of bad luck, we had the affair Dino Fumo – which as far as Mr A was concerned, set back Anglo-European relations about a decade.

He'd strolled down ahead of me one evening into the unspoilt fishing village of Noli – I say strolled, but actually you backed down sideways against the sea wall, our hotel being on the main coast road, or Via Aurelia, if you want to get fancy, from Italy into France, and a two-way interchange of motorists at high speed all round the clock, with hooting, flashing headlights and rude shouts out of the windows . . . it was a new hotel, and he'd left me behind to complain that the only illumination we'd got in our room was bare wires coming out of holes in the wall, and the promised bolt for the door still hadn't come from Genoa – are you with me all right? Good. He'd strolled down to our chosen unspoilt waterfront cafe, the Cafe Sorrento, no less – they're very conservative about names. We'd chosen it because it hadn't got an unspoilt TV set. Not that it made a lot of difference, because the joints either side had got one, and the joints beyond them, in both directions, until they tailed off under the blue Italian night into depressed areas still rubbing along with old-fashioned juke boxes and the occasional local beat group. You were more or less in the eye of the hurricane at the Sorrento, lots of turbulence all around but none of it actually hitting you.

The great drawback with that holiday was that we couldn't blame it on any of our friends, and not even on each other, because it was an agency recommendation. Still, now I come to think of it, Jack and Julie Sheldrake recommended the agency, so I suppose we could get them on that, if the statute of limitations hasn't set in. It was one of those simply marvellous little one-man agencies, old man, that use the word unspoilt like commas . . . and if you hadn't already taken your statements on agency practice and performance, I could go on pouring the stuff into you like cornflakes.

Well, as it later transpired, Mr A was sitting there, thinking how much cheaper it would be at home, with a chair on the back lawn and no uproar but the chaffinches, when up breezed this laughing, sixteen-stone Italian, holding out a hand and bawling 'Dino Fumo!' – which caused Mr A to say that he was frightfully sorry and put his cigarette out. When the smiling, plain-clothes Mafia close in like this, and tell you it's no smoking, you lose no time playing along; anyway, not on Mr A's side of the marriage.

Nothing of the kind, it turned out. Mr A's idea of interpreting a foreign language is to pick out the words that sound anything like English and act accordingly. This Fumo, in fact, was only announcing his nice, easy name, and when Mr A cottoned on it suited him fine. If he'd been called Giacinto Ricciulli Sagramola things could have gone differently. As it was, when I got down there, unmarked unless you count a trace of tyre tread across one shoe, they were getting along like a burning varnish factory.

Signor Fumo, as he wouldn't let us call him, hadn't a lot of English; about as much as makes you feel sorry for foreigners on a London bus. But it made my Italian not worth bothering with, and Mr A's look like a speck on the wall. He builds up a vocabulary very slowly, does Mr A, about five words a year, and even then he only retains them by a supreme effort, or if they've been particularly impressed on him by circumstances at the time. It's also a danger when he learns two words on the same day. On our honeymoon in far-flung Dieppe, he learnt 'pretty' and 'kind', but he was always telling terrible old men in the market that they were very pretty, and their sense of fun often wasn't up to it. It happened again in Italy this time, with carabinieri and zabaglione: then when he tells the waiter that he doesn't fancy cheese tonight, can't he have an armed policeman instead, and the man falls about and rushes off to share the fun with the kitchen staff, he goes into a sulk and won't throw a prego to a dog for the next three days.

You don't get this sort of thing with the foreigners. Two words of English and they'd polish it on the nearest tourist's three-year-old tot. What English he had, Dino was mad keen on speaking, and even though rich topics like gasket-cement and powered steering weren't on, and he said worry for hurry and feet instead of hands, there's no doubt that he brought that breath of home that you need in a distant land, after three days trying to hit the right word for wasps or funny smell in the shower-bath. So I could see Mr A was indulgently inclined. Italians with this much civilized vocabulary must have some good in them, especially when, as in Dino's case, they've been sunk off Taranto by the Royal Navy and tell you about it with shouts of reminiscent laughter. 'They were great day,' roared Dino, mopping his eyes and accepting another large Scotch at unspoilt Italian prices. He rose, bowed, and clinked our glasses.

'You are friends?'

'Married,' said Mr A.

'He means are we his friends, you dope.'

'Si, si,' said Mr A. 'Si, si, si, si.' And, getting carried away. 'Si, si, si, si, si, si.'

It soon seemed established that we were. Dino wasn't the negotiator I'd have picked, myself, but I don't mind admitting that at this point it looked a cinch that I was on to another chance of getting Mr A into Europe. But it was not (sighed Mrs A), as they say, to be.

'What wasn't?' Mr A had entered eating some sort of small bun, and carrying others. 'What do you call these things?'

'You know perfectly well,' said Mrs A. 'You were the one who read the recipe to me aloud, in a strained voice, when the Captain told us there was low cloud at Heathrow.'

'They explode like hand grenades. It's going to take all afternoon to get the currants out of the projector.'

'Leave him within a mile of an unlocked cake tin,' said Mrs A, 'and you'd think the white ants were here. How many have you had? They were supposed to be for the tea adjournment.'

'Wouldn't you think that a woman – "Magical Minutes", are they called? – You'd think, wouldn't you, that a woman still living out of suitcases forty-eight hours after touchdown would be upstairs at the chest of drawers of an evening, instead of slogging out a batch of buns with comic names that happened to take her eye five miles up over Cherbourg? "Moments Musicaux", is it?'

'I suppose he won't be happy till I say it. It isn't my fault what the cookery journalists think up. Melting Moments, as you know damned well.'

'Ha-ha,' said Mr A. 'Try one, only watch the fragmentation.'

Q. May I?

'And if I were you,' said Mrs A, 'I'd lay off the foreign language bit just at this time. I was in the middle of making a statement about the mess it got us into with your friend Dino Fumo, the Ligurian dynamo and entrepreneur.'

'If that's the line she's giving you,' said Mr A, 'I'd like to say two things. First that you can probably get her on a perjury charge. And second, that I think you'd do well to put me on the stand instead, while she haggles with the man who's called about the prefabricated greenhouse.'

'What? And he swore to telephone first, on his glazier's honour.' She picked her way swiftly from the disordered courtroom.

When (said Mr A, shrugging) will they ever learn? Have another of these things, they're not half bad.

Q. *Thank you. On a point not strictly relevant to the present enquiry, though with some bearing on the wider view of the married state, don't you find it highly gratifying that your wife should be willing to receive prefabricated greenhouse men, and with such meekness and dispatch?*

A. *Highly. On the other hand, she needed to get out quick before I mentioned that this was the first I'd heard about any greenhouse and asked what she was damn well playing at, with the funds down to zero and the last bird-table not paid for yet.*

Q. *You would have mentioned that?*

A. *And have her hunting through the files for my new tape-recorder receipt? Some of us learn a thing or two, with the passing years of union. I'd like to put a question to you now.*

Q. *About what?*

A. *About what was not to be.*

Q. *I beg your pardon?*

A. *When I came in. She was saying that something was not to be.*

Q. *Ah. A hoped-for rapprochement between you and the Europeans, Mr A. Some piece of Italian evidence. I wonder whether you'd care to take up at the meeting with your friend Dino – er – Fumo?*

It's not my place (said Mr A) to warn you against a too easy acceptance of everything you hear, but you want to watch it, all the same. There was no question, of course, of his being my friend. She was on to him like a bird on a bacon rind, just because she could keep her phrase-book in her handbag for once. And since a man likes to see a wife happy, within reason, I naturally played along, and this despite an experience with a Dutch television producer we met in Amsterdam last year, who offered to show her round the studio wardrobe and let her try on some of the costumes while I was in The Hague arranging an over-thirties cricket fixture. Perhaps you don't know it, but there are more MCC and Free Foresters' ties in The Hague than you'd find on a bus to the Oval in mid-July. Very cunning players, too. They stuff the opposing team with a thirty-six dish blowout the night before, and when you get to the wicket you've got bits of savoury rice coming out of your eyeballs and can't tell middle-and-leg from Old Trafford. I wouldn't mention this at all, except that when our lot went over and played this game Mrs A wouldn't even come and be scorer – and that from a girl who insists that the fun of foreign travel is all in learning the language. In fact, the only thing she asked me when I got back was the Dutch for LBW. Which I could tell her, luckily.

Q. *What is it?*
A. *LBW.*
Q. *Ah. Would you now care to continue with the Italian evidence?*

We only knew Dino for two days (said Mr A). It seems longer, looking back. In a different society I suppose you'd have said he was the village headman. He had a little seafront office about the size of one of those stick-on sun loggias in the lower price range, labelled with the Italian for estate agent, which I can't call to mind at the moment, and a wealth of sidelines in boat-trips, taxi-hire, foreign exchange, tourist accommodation, camping sites, lottery tickets, interpreting, getting you out of your military service, consular representation and drying anybody's wet bathing costume if they cared to pop in and leave it in the sun on the typewriter. He never seemed to be engaged in any of this work, though, because he had to give up a lot of time to being a leader of cafe society, drinking Scotch and joining in the sound-track of very loud operatic gramophone records. We didn't find out a lot of this, especially the gramophone records, until our association was well ripened, getting on towards about midnight on the evening we met. This was in a cafe called the Cafe Salerno, like most of the cafes along there. He suddenly sprang up and kissed a hand to himself and yelled, 'I am remember! Is Dino's birthday tonight, we having office party!' The office was only a bottle's throw along the front, open to the night and all the lights on, so it was no trouble making it. I was all for bed, myself, but you know what wives are. Anything rich and strange in foreign parts — like an office party they wouldn't go to at home if you dragged them there in a gold coach — and you can't keep them away and save the marriage.

No, the trouble was actually squeezing us into the place, because on the way there he'd mopped up anybody in sight not having the look of a prior engagement; this made about twenty-two in all, including a man who did rope-tricks and a sort of old Ligurian hill-billy who'd been serenading the Salerno customers with bagpipes made out of a patched inner tube, so Dino had to force us through the door like an underground porter at the rush hour. In fact, Schwanda the Bagpiper had to leave his instrument outside, the first time round, while we wedged ourselves in among the filing cabinets and tottering stacks of Come to Sunny Italy handouts. But by the time the corks were popping, and *Tosca* was belting clean out over the Gulf of Genoa and waking them up on Elba, he'd recovered it from some kids who were off down the beach with it for a moonlight swim and brought it back inside. Also the kids. I think they may have been Dino's. They bashed around for a time with rubber stamps and stapling machines and then disappeared, either got trampled or trapped in desk knee-holes: or, now I come to think of it, a rather dejected sort of woman in black put her head through a communicating door a couple of times and went away like Anna Magnani after bad news. She could have scooped them to safety. Office parties were nothing new to her, I'd have said, even with Dino and the inner-tuber both supporting the chap who was singing Scarpia every time he hit the grooves. I must admit it was just as well we hadn't gone to bed — I like to concede a point when I can: our hotel wasn't half a mile off, and it would have been like stretching out under the stage at La Scala, Milan. I thought the authorities were on to us once, when a couple of zabaglioni arrived in the doorway, shouting and —

Q. Er — . Oh, it's all right. Yes?

Couple of cops with revolvers, shouting and waving. I could see the headlines. Britons in Italian Vice Swoop. I had an interesting mental throwback to days of former glory, and felt in my jacket pocket for the passports, with that bit in the front warning foreigners not to lay a finger on us or else. However, I couldn't find them, and I couldn't even find the jacket, to be perfectly frank. Mixing lachryma Christi with a form of gin from a bottle labelled London Fizz can blunt the perceptions. It wouldn't be overstating things to say that a drowsy numbness pained my sense, even with somebody taking flashlight polaroids all the time and dealing them round like cards.

Q. *Would any of these photographs be available to produce in evidence?*
A. *You could bind and gag us and search the albums. It's a matter of whether you have the time to waste.*
Q. *Yes. Could you pick up at the police raid, please?*

I was wrong about that. It was purely social. They squeezed in and shook what hands they could reach, had a drink and a smoke and the overture to *Aida*, and moved on, satisfied that no disturbance was being caused. I must say, it gave me some idea of what Mussolini was up against, getting that lot to march in step, and you can see why he went too far in the end, with a challenging exercise like that.

In any case, vice didn't come into it. Granted there were a few girls there, and I felt I knew one of them quite well. Either she was the spitting image, as they say, of Claudia Cardinale, or the assistant attendant at the Gents just along the beach. This was never established, because by that time we'd got to act two, scene two of *Aida*, and Dino was leading us in song from the top of his desk, treading the orders-to-view underfoot and conducting with his shirt. I don't want to be boastful, but I think I can claim to have gone along with things quite well, and it wouldn't have hurt Mrs A to say an appreciative word, when you consider she's always complaining that I act standoffishly with the alien peasantry.

It was a night. The trick, as with all parties, and especially one with three people to the square yard, was getting to the door. I practically had to cut us free with oxy-acetylene gear, and even then she had to go back for something, as usual. And I can't say I was too pleased to hear the next morning that she'd accepted a further invitation for that very afternoon. They take with both hands, that's their trouble. Nor did I feel, even after a crash course of Alka-Seltzer and sitting motionless on the edge of the bed, that she needed to keep harping on a hot chicken tea.

'What hot chicken tea?' I forced myself to ask.

'Up in the mountains. We're going to have this lovely hot chicken tea. Then see Dino's new villa. I don't know what to wear.'

An inexperienced husband could have said You never do, at a time like this, and wished he'd counted up to five first. I was still counting when she was off again.

'You don't help me,' she said. 'What do I go in? You get all creased on these long car rides.'

'Four, five,' I said. 'Talking of creases, something very extraordinary seems to have happened to my jacket in the night.' It had grown a bunch of tight vertical pleats round the middle, giving an old-fashioned corn-stock effect, but irregular. 'It can't be insects, even in this hotel. What long car rides?'

'Long car rides to eat lovely hot chicken teas.'

'I don't know what you're talking about.'

'You ought to. You fixed it. Couldn't talk about anything else last night.' She went out on the balcony and filled her lungs luxuriously with carbon monoxide and diesel fumes.

'Come back in off there, I can't hear you for the traffic.'

'It's going to be a scorcher,' she said. 'Especially about teatime, when we have the hot —'

'Look. One more mention of — '

'I shall wear my pink top and lemon pants.'

'What villa?'

'Dino's villa. You're the one he fixed it up with. You had it all — '

'I most certainly — '

' — all pat enough last night. Take-off two o'clock, cars at the door. Tea in the mountains. See Dino's new villa, back for dinner.'

'Is this a joke?' I said — because at times like these a marriage can find itself borrowing dialogue from stage and screen, and feels low about it. 'I recall no such arrangements being made. Absolutely.'

'I don't suppose you do. I don't suppose you recall trying to make the words of Drink to me Only fit the Soldiers' Chorus from Faust. Or betting the rope-trick man that he couldn't pull his reef knots out straight with your jacket tied in them.'

'If there were one word of truth — '

'All right, it's insects. I'm pressing this button here that says Valet, OK? And a picture of a matchstick man with some trousers over his arm. I suppose they do jackets as well. You'll want to look nice for the hot chicken tea — '

'Excuse me.' Even with his stomach heaving like an obstacle race under a tarpaulin a man tries to remember his manners. She came and hammered on the bathroom door.

'Besides,' she yelled, 'next time it gets chilly at three in the morning, and you want to put your jacket round some early developer you've been calling Claudia all night, while I'm chattering my teeth in the back-lash from an improvised bagpipes . . . '

Oh, indeed, it was a neat job she'd done. As I was saying a minute or two back, I like to concede a point when I can. Even the ranks of Tuscany, on occasion, can scarce forbear to cheer. Not that I advise cheering. It's possible to concede too much. But armed resistance must be ruled out absolutely at these times. Disaster ensues. Ronald and Sylvia Dinsdale, who used to be friends of ours before they forked off in different directions after a similar situation at Positano, forgot this. It started from nothing, a mere comment by Sylvia that he'd helped to fix the beach umbrellas of five different girls in their first week, while she had to fix her own and kept trapping her wrist in the spokes; he said so what, it wasn't as if he'd fixed the same girl's umbrella five times: she said she wouldn't put it past him, any day she decided to stay indoors with her sunburn; he said did she think he hadn't noticed how she kept shifting her Li-lo so that she could twinkle at a nearby slab of beefcake in mock lion-skin trunks; she said – but never mind, you see the way things were going, and in the end they were beating each other with bedlamps. The greatest of married holiday hazards is that there's all the time in the world to discuss things, and no guillotine on the debates.

When I came out, some relief having been afforded, Mrs A just said, 'Better?'

'Fine,' I said.

'You weren't absolutely clear last night,' she said, stepping into the lemon pants and as steady as a rock even on one leg, 'whether it's a tea where we actually eat hot chicken, or something in cups, like beef tea but it's not beef, you know?'

Mussolini all over again. They never know when to stop, and the knock at the door was happily timed. A man came in with a tray.

'Prego. You ringing for drink?'

As one, we decided that we had been, actually.

'Con ghiaccio,' she said. Whatever it meant they were a big success.

Later, when we were halfway down them, I thanked her for going back for my jacket. It took real devotion, I said, going back into that lot.

'I am devoted,' she said. 'Besides, it was fun stripping it off her.'

Anyone who can't get his marriage going on lines of true frankness, and with no more rancour that you could fit under a mosquito's tail feathers, should join some good anti-Anti-Temperance body, if you ask me.

One thing I'll hand the Latins (resumed Mr A) is their phenomenal rate of bob-up. If I'd been in Dino's boots after that party I should have been dead for two days from the singing alone. Nothing of the sort. When he rolled up that afternoon, prompt on the stroke of two-thirty, with a purple silk suit and –

Q. *According to my notes – I want to avoid any inaccuracies – wasn't he expected at two?*

A. *Prompt at two thirty is two, with the Latins.*

Q. *I see. Yes?*

– and two old Fiats specially flown over from the Montagu motor museum, he looked like a man who'd been a week at a health farm. We'd given him up. We were out on a back balcony, comparing headache notes, when his merry laugh rang clean through the building like a knell.

The cars were well down on their springs already. Space for one had been left in the second car; that was for us two, with Anna Magnani, a mother, father, two brothers-in-law, all dressed for a funeral and cold March winds –

Q. *Wasn't this in the summer time?*

A. *That's right. Ninety in the shade.*

Q. *Thank you. Yes?*

– and a driver in an off-white singlet and a six months' beard. But this was only because he hadn't started to shave yet; he just should have done. He was pushing seventeen, at a guess, and must have lied about his age to get his licence, probably with a bit of influence by Dino. Exuberance is the word that comes to mind for him, and it came more and more when we finally went roaring off into the unadopted by-ways.

If you've ever been driven up the foothills of the Apennines under these conditions you'll know what it's like, and won't want reminding. Mrs A and I were packed close enough for thought transference by touch, and the thoughts we transferred were, roughly, just how far would we somersault down the sheer drops on either side when we actually came off the road? There were trees below us, it's true, sticking out of the mountain sideways, but they were poor things with an undernourished, flexible look. Might stop a lightish scooter, but no real threat to a ton and a half of horseless carriage ballasted by Dino's relations. We should go the distance, was our unspoken view, and the question was, when the Gulf of Genoa closed over us, would an Eyeteye coastguard, if there are such things, give priority to fishing out his own nationals before throwing a line to a pair of aliens?

During a statutory pause midway up when our driver took on half a bottle of bianco to make good his outgoings, and showed us the creased photograph of Fangio he carried as a mascot, we had further thoughts, namely, what was it going to be like coming down? At present, we at least had gravity working for us. Coming down, the singlet further fortified, the gradient backing him to the hilt, and the brake-linings down to a frayed wisp, we shouldn't just come off the road and drop, we should fly out into mid-Gulf like a bolas and sink in forty fathoms.

Dino, packed tight by girls, also a man with a faintly legal look, was driving the car in front, so we got a few yards' warning to brace ourselves for the deeper holes. When we saw his lot hitting the roof we could hang on to the under-side of the seat. We escaped major concussions in this way. The family didn't bother, just bounced up and hit, their hands folded. They were only there, we decided later, to lend the trip a semblance of economics, occupying seats that would otherwise have been wasted. They retained their composure as we rounded a final hairpin and our bald, locked tyres slid to a halt.

'Thank God,' said Mrs A, and, coming out of it, yelled through the window, 'Lovely! Bella, bella! Dino lucky man!'

'Why do you have to speak broken English?' I said. When nerves are taut they find relief in this sort of thing.

'You speak some, you dope,' she said.

'Très fortunato!' I said.

Dino, leaving his car a moment or two before it came to rest, had hurried back to us, huge, hot, beaming, and eager for praise. Simple fellow. Endearing really. The 'villa', which had a good fire going, judging by its column of black chimney smoke, looked like a prefabricated breeze-block garage in poor repair. As we poured out of the cars into the refreshing coolness of the upper Fahrenheits he swept an operatic gesture towards it.

'Hot chicken tea!'

It wasn't the villa at all, but some inexplicable outpost of the catering industry, the proprietor now bowing in the doorway over his blacked apron. Discussing it since, we've often worried about how it got its supplies. It was a long way from the shops. It must have got them somehow, because there were fifteen of us and we had a chicken each. They were smallish, but more than adequate. Also a bottle of bianco. Each. That included our driver. I had to barge a bit, and possibly appear somewhat unmannerly, but I got the seat next to him, and twice when his attention was distracted, I hid his bottle under the table. But Dino wasn't going to see anyone die of thirst and sent down instant replacements. We had some words about it afterwards. Mrs A said it was my worst stratagem since Monte Carlo, where I affected a limp to get seats on a bus and was knocked into a tobacco kiosk as soon as the other contender saw I was handicapped. The downy-jowled delinquent, she said, could have been kept down to a bottle if I hadn't tried anything on. As things were, he must have ended up with a good two and a half.

There were toasts. The family, who could see themselves footing the bill, I shouldn't wonder, were abstemious, but acknowledged our raised glasses with sullen nods.

The villa was within walking distance, a hundred yards down a boulder-strewn track. The big surprise about it, as Dino flung out his arms to embrace the small clearing in the woods, was that it wasn't there. Nothing. Trouble with the language-barrier again. With Dino's O-Level English, the distinction between a site for a villa and an actual villa had been easy to blur. Hard to say the right thing really, looking at the tree stumps and slaughtered shrubbery which now turned out to be the object of the whole distressing exercise. All around were the sun-scorched hills. The family stood in line, waiting for the good word. I came in, I think I can say, bang on cue.

'Bella vista!'

It went big. Even Mrs A gave me a look of guarded admiration. The whole company took it up, even the brothers-in-law. 'Bella vista, bella vista!' The name of a house in Chertsey, Cheltenham, Bolton, Lechlade, Coventry, Fishguard and anywhere else you care to name rang round the welkin like a battle cry.

Which is roughly what it turned out to be, we found a few minutes later. Anyway, I did. Dino, herding the rest of them back to the cars, drew me and the Lincoln's Inn type towards the tea shack.

'Now what?' I said to Mrs A, on a dwindling note.

'Search me.'

A marriage is a partnership. I felt seriously alone as the three of us sat at the grease-splashed table, fumes from the faded feast settling heavily around us. Even when Dino's associate drew a parchment from his inner pocket I still wasn't with it.

Being in shock (said Mr A) I don't recall much about the drive back. It must have been hell. Mrs A hadn't had the blow at first hand, of course, so she claims to remember several involuntary short cuts through copses and thickets on most of the snakier bends. I missed them myself. We weren't taken back to the hotel, just flung out in mid-village and left to find our own way home. No farewells were exchanged, or even words of any kind, in any tongue. The family's lips had disappeared, so they were speechless anyway. It even seemed unsuitable, somehow, to thank Dino for his hospitality, which I must say, in spite of everything, I hope he got back off his income tax. He could, if anyone could, I should think. But it hardly seems likely, with no sale. How was I to know I was supposed to buy a dozen roods of clearing in the foothills of the Apennines?

I put the point to Mrs A.

'You could learn the bloody language,' she said.

It's very, very seldom – and I'd be obliged if you'd make a note – that we swear at each other. At any rate, when the other one's there.

X

'Let there be an end, a privacy,
an obscure nook for me.'
Robert Browning

'I SHOULD have thought,' said Mrs A, appearing through the hydrangeas with tall glasses for three and some assorted cushions, 'that if the court turned up its last notebook but about six, it would quite easily find our offer of voluntary statements on the foreign water closet wherever it is to be found.'

'Which it mostly can't be.' Mr A was lying prone on an oil-stained air bed, giving it the kiss of life. 'And I don't see why you call it that, really, considering the only water – Why won't this thing blow up?'

'Have some ice.'

'Yes, please.'

'Not you,' said Mrs A.

Q. *Thank you very much. May I just ask where* – ?

'I thought he knew where,' said Mrs A.

'He'll have to go into the house,' said Mr A, panting.

'We keep meaning to have one down past the toolshed. It's the first thing jobbing gardeners want to know these days.'

'Even,' gasped Mr A, 'before the money or the powered hedge cutter. Why is this thing killing me?'

Q. *May I just ask where the proposed statement, voluntary or otherwise, impinges on the present enquiry?*

'It's elementary dynamics, you dope, if I've got that right.' Mrs A reclined abruptly on the cushions. 'You can't expect two tiny lungs to raise an eleven stone man four inches. You'll get those red and black eye-fireworks again. Why don't you pump it with the foot puffer?'

'If you remember, you made me leave the foot puffer at La Baule airport, panicking over excess baggage weight. Also anything else we could unpack that I was fond of, such as my wool fisherman's hat from La Rochelle with the tassel on top.'

'It got us – '

'And my – '

'At least it got us through without paying.'

'Only because they didn't weigh anything that flight. On one of their whims. If they had, your "All-New Fannie Farmer Boston Cooking School Cookbook" would have been enough to sink us. The one you bought in Rheims. Where the jackdaws come from.'

'Why drag them in?'

'They collect a lot of junk, too.'

'Casting your mind back to a bookstall in Constitution Square, Athens,' said Mrs A, coldly, 'you may recall being so starved for a line of English print that you blew a hundred and twenty-five drachs on "Arthritis and Folk Medicine," by a Dr D. C. Jarvis.'

Q. Could I just – ?

'Besides, I was thinking,' said Mrs A. 'If you ever get that thing inflated, we ought to let the court have it, instead of that spastic deck chair, which is going to ruin its dignity if it folds up under it.'

Q. *Please. Could the court just make a suggestion? Namely, that we regard this as more of an informal convening, the witnesses being given, so to speak, free range, and the court merely noting any relevancies, if so deemed, as may arise?*

You could deem two, for a kick-off, funnily enough (said Mrs A). It was at La Rochelle that we had the Case of the Running Nun, and La Baule airport was where we headed a queue outside a door that said *occupé* when it was really *libre*. It was only when an airline official jumped the queue and went in anyway, that we found they'd got the bolt on back to front, thus misleading the public. It was too late then, they'd called our flight twice, and Mr A said if he had to run he'd never make it. Very unusual, for the French, though – when we all sprang out of our seat belts after take-off, and lined up for the tail, they respected the precedences from the queue on the ground. But that's it, of course, that's what flying does for people. When they're airborne they always go to town on the courtesies. They don't like to tempt Providence with anything it could take reprisals for, which it's naturally in a strong position to do up there.

The latch disaster at La Baule was only a culmination, as it happens, and this made it more painful. In every way. I don't know whether you're acquainted with La Baule airport? Probably not. It's very elusive, and I don't know how the pilots find it, because we couldn't. If my lawful wedded booby could get it through his skull – I beg your pardon? Don't worry, he's asleep; he always shows a little slit of eye-white like that, I've got used to it now, but I don't mind saying it shook me on the honeymoon – No, he still has this idea that airports are near the places they're named after. At least he's learnt where London's is by now, and doesn't go looking for it round Oxford Circus any more, but he still hasn't corrected for foreign parts. What with this, and a terrible restlessness about clocks, there's nothing you can suggest to him, from about an hour before dawn on the day of flight, that he doesn't yell, 'Just forget it, will you? We can do it at the airport.' And he throws all the bags in the car with face-cloths hanging out, and we're away, with his window open listening for jets warming up that are about eighteen miles off. I shall have to tell you later about La Baule proper, because it – Sorry? Yes, extremely relevant; as I was just going to say, it was the scene of the Great Wet Seat Mystery – But the unique thing about the airport is that it's the only one he ever got me to that wasn't even open yet. It was very depressing for him, because he'd waved all plans aside, saying that once we made it we could shop there, eat there, drink there, take the tranquillizers and everything. Particularly the everything. We'd even left without breakfast, he was so eager for the off, just a gallon of coffee, so naturally we hadn't . . . However. On the way out of the town I'd shown him a sign saying Hommes and he wouldn't look at it. He's never good with other people's suggestions. Then about ten miles on there was another, and by this time he was coming round to the idea slightly so he got out and looked, and was back like a boomerang saying that it said Hommes but it was only a Dames – and with a pretty black look, in fact.

It's the sort of thing that doesn't come out much in dinner-table conversation, but lots of marriages show their first cracks on this, the conviction, if you're a Dame, that the Homme gets twice the official provision you do; and if you're an Homme, of course, vice versa. It may sound a small point, but you have to remember it always comes up when the parties are under strain already, or one of them at least. With this particular little rusty French loo he probably only needed to walk round the other side, but he has this shy streak, doesn't like to be seen prospecting for the obvious; also, to be fair, there's some sort of peculiar blind spot in his direction-finder. He's always lost at sea, for instance. Once on a Dutch boat called the *Oranje* he got completely fixed on a route, like a tram, and every time he set off for the amenities he ended up coming in the First Officer's cabin by a side entrance. They had to close a watertight door just along the corridor to cut him off, until he got orientated, and even then I had to go and find it for him for three days, like an Indian scout.

And that's another thing, just for the record. There's nothing in the text of the well-known Solemnization, as I remember it, saying the bride shall be the one to find the lavs all her life. But ask any girl who's seen a couple of years' service. She'll tell you that the late groom, arriving at the Hotel Bristol anywhere from Reykjavik to Brazilia, will sit around in keen discomfort, probably aggravating things with a small Scotch (no water), while his child-wife goes padding off on the vital mission for two. And when she comes back all she gets is, 'Right. Where's mine?' And he can hardly wait for a rough sketch-map on the inside of the book matches before he's off at the cautious trot, leaving her to buy her own drink. I often wonder whether the marriage guidance people ever open up this field. My advice for a husband admitting to major breaches, such as strangers regularly bringing him home dead stoned and smelling of alien perfume, but who nevertheless wants a reconciliation and many happy years together, would be three little words. Find the Ladies. It doesn't sound much, but four wives out of five would grab it in full and sufficient settlement. And if, having found it, and it turns out to be a Gents too, which can happen to the traveller in an antique land – and in Yugoslavia there can be goats in there as well – if he then goes and brings her tenderly by the hand, instead of dashing in first and wedging the door shut with his air-mail *Daily Telegraph*, he qualifies for the Galahad Star of Chivalry, with Crossed Legs – sorry, Swords, I mean –

Q. H'm. *Could we* – ?

– and possibly the Order of Gunga Din, with Moist Palms. Ha-ha. I couldn't stop, sorry.

Q. *Yes. Are we now* – ?

Just a further point strikes me, though; about those all-purpose comfort stations that simply say Toilet and no segregation of the sexes. I always think it's curious, the way you can rush in regardless, all boys and girls together, an exercise in non-discrimination that would have made Emmeline Pankhurst's life a song. But when they split them into separates, as they often do, even in another town in the same country, a Dame only has to get into the Hommes, or the other way round, and the gnarled attendant is practically hobbling off for the vice squad. Have another drink?

Q. *At the moment, no. Are we now, I was going to ask, within sight of La Baule airport?*

Not really (said Mrs A). And I may as well tell you, as to all intents and purposes we're alone, that I wished I'd checked on that particular Dames in person, because after another fifteen miles or thereabouts, and still no sign of the airport, except signs saying Airport, I was beginning to get, well, hungry, for one thing. The terrain wasn't helpful, in the circumstances. Either very open, featureless to the horizon with no cover but wire fences, or sudden blocks of industrial buildings that had no sort of air of welcome about them, somehow, for a couple of foreigners screeching to a halt outside and saying they'd like a wash. During the next stretch of indescribably unvegetated countryside something rather distrubing happened. The signs saying Airport stopped, which could only mean we'd missed it. I don't know how. Airports take some missing, even for Mr A. Put yourself in my place, though, and you'll realize that comment would have been unwise. He may be a semi-idiot, with a bump of location the size of countersunk rivet, but I think – if he were awake – even he would admit to a planning failure when you're expecting a vista of windsock and tarmac and instead you suddenly have to stand on everything so as not to hit a ship. Because this is what happened next. A king-size docks loomed up out of the target area and closed in on us with cranes, steam-hammering and French sailors, one of whom put an admittedly small bayonet through the open window.

'Ask him for the airport, quick,' said Mr A.

'The airport, quick,' I said.

'Tell him we've got to catch a plane in – what's the time now? – less than four hours.'

One thing about being an unpaid interpreter, you needn't interpret if you don't want to. As the airport was a mere two miles back, and only an idiot could have missed the turn-off, any hint of time pressing, with four hours in hand, could have landed us in the Bastille on suspicion. As it was, he let us turn round and go, with a long, Gallic shrug in the rear view mirror. Ah! the English.

St Nazaire, that's where we'd got to, and for a nasty moment or two it looked as if we might have to go home by submarine.

The one thing everyone says about airports, even people who've never seen one, is that they all look alike (continued Mrs A). All I can say is, they don't know La Baule, do they, darling, I hope you realize you've been sleeping during the hearing?

'I heard the whole thing,' said Mr A, reaching for the cheese straws with his foot.

'You didn't hear my evidence about that day in Crete, when she wouldn't show me where it was until I'd eaten a plate of buns, and you were –'

'Every word.'

'You're making a very bad impression on the court, saying that, because I haven't even mentioned Crete yet.'

'Anyway,' said Mr A, yielding ground in good order, 'that was my joke at St Nazaire. I was the one who said about going home by submarine. And you trot it out as if you'd just minted it.'

Q. *Would you perhaps care to take the stand, Mr A, as you are now once more –*
er – ?

The Great Wet Seat Mystery (said Mr A), happened the same year as the Case of the Running Nun, and we'd have put them both up to Erle Stanley Gardner's agent if they hadn't taken off the Perry Masons just about then and put Ray Burr in a wheel chair.

It's a great feature of the motoring holiday, of course, that you can shop around for your accommodation. None of that leaving the bags piled against a kebab-stand or traffic-cop's rostrum and flat-footing it round the Michelin list. The hotel we'd picked for La Baule was called the Brighton. I think we were getting a bit homesick by then. It was a no-star hotel – and I hope you'll take our references to foreign high life with a pinch of marines, by the way. We've been on holidays before now where we didn't see any stars at all except through cracks in the ceiling. There'd been plenty of time to pick it, while we were pulled in to the side of the N.771, steamed-up and with the lights on, in a confluence of cloud-bursts, but by the time we'd cast off, pumped the car out and breasted the tide into La Baule only a few clouds were still bursting and visibility was a good five yards, if you stuck to one eye at a time while the other was drying out.

It was late, therefore, on this wringing summer evening when I eased myself out of the driving seat into the shallow end of the Avenue of the Pelicans, or it may have been Nightingales, I'm not sure. What we really wanted was the Avenue of the Eagles, I think. Possibly the Spoonbills. They were all in this estate laid out by some speculative bird-lover in about 1932. You can only guess at these things but I'd say he'd hired a man to design a large half-timbered residence, doomed from its very blueprint to lapse into a guest-house, with marble steps up to a patio where the front door should have been, but there were only French windows into an empty dining-room with a sideboard full of cruets. And he built it a hundred and eighty times in the middle of a dripping pinewood, all in little short avenues cleverly angled to keep vulgar parallels off the drawing board at all costs. This meant that if you splashed up the Flamingoes and turned down the Woodpeckers expecting to come into the Curlews, what you actually hit was the Pelicans again, and Mrs A with her lips at the car window crack saying, 'You insisted on a twin-bedded room?' And you spirting rain like a water pistol and saying 'The way things are going you'll be lucky to sleep on a piano.' When I'd been back three times, and nowhere nearer the Brighton than Hastings and St Leonards, we agreed on a hoot every five minutes, so that when I heard it I could sheer off in a direction where it got fainter. It was about an hour before I made landfall, and dark by then; it wasn't easy to read the street and house names by a dying cigarette lighter, especially as the seeping pines kept scoring a bull on its wick. What's more, tomorrow was garbage day, and the bins were out, so that was another hazard. Still, it kept Mrs A in touch: at least she could pinpoint me by the crashes.

But I don't wish in any way to harrow the court. I found the Brighton in the end. It was in the Eagles, all right, but its front door was round the side in the Waxwings. The landlady, who had posed when younger for that Keep Death off the Road poster showed me a room I'd taken before she'd even turned the handle, and as we were both starving I went straight into the 'When's dinner?'

No dinner, she said. She looked quite affronted. No catering of any kind. Just a roof. So, to cut a long voyage short, we ended up at the Sandringham. Avenue of the Cormorants, and you can say that again, with cold bathwater, yesterday's bread, a hundred and ninety francs for two nights and find your own lunch. Not forgetting the Wet Seat Mystery.

The room they gave us had a private bathroom attached. It was the only room free, they said, which didn't strike us as funny until dinner, when ours turned out to be the only laid table in twenty-four. I think something had slipped up with the conversion plan, because it was really more a bathroom with a bedroom attached, and for a time we discussed moving the sleeping arrangements in there, where there was an acre to spare, and we could have got into bed without bruising our knees on the wall. When you think of the times when you'd give your pension rights for a private bathroom – and there we were, this time, stuck with one we didn't want, at the end of a spent-up fortnight with nothing in reserve but a hundred francs accidentally wedged behind Mrs A's handbag lining . . .

At first, naturally, we weren't surprised to find the seat wet. What wasn't, that day? Either the hotel leaked, or I'd accidentally emptied my raincoat pockets on it. But it was wet again after dinner, and again before breakfast. And again after. The hotel towels weren't up to much; if you held them to the light they looked like old Bisley targets, so we were soon drying out with vests and pants. The leak theory was off next day, because it was sunny and dry, but everytime we went in there it was wet again all the same.

I was the one who solved it. Even if she was awake – you'll notice, by the way, she's got her knees stuck up in a lumpy posture she swears she never sleeps in – she wouldn't deny that. I was there. Sitting reading Figaro, the latest on a night club hostess found at the Gare de Lyon in several cardboard boxes. The phantom showed its hand, drenching me from below. It was a severe nervous shock, as a matter of fact, and Mrs A came banging on the door asking why I'd screamed.

'Well, you know the volcanic island of Santorini – ?'

Q. *I've heard of it. Yes?*

I'm glad someone's awake, but I wasn't talking to the court, actually. I don't think it always listens for the quotation marks.

'You know the volcanic island,' I said to her through chattering teeth, 'of Santorini?'

'I've heard of it,' she said. 'Yes?'

'You've not only heard of it, you've been there,' I said.

'And what's so funny?'

I then explained, handing her my shirt to wring out, that in Agios Nikolaos, in Crete –

'I've been there,' she said.

They've no idea when a thing's beside the point.

In Agios Nikolaos, in the middle of the village, there's an ice-cold, bottomless pool. And they say that when there's an eruption on Santorini, which is often enough for at least two people I know to stay aboard the cruise ship, anchored well out, and leave the rest of the passenger-list to climb it by mule and come back reeking of hot lava, there's a tumultuous waterspout in this pool in Crete, getting on for two hundred miles away. Something of this kind, I told her, obviously kept happening in the Hotel Brighton, Avenue des Cormorans. At some distant spot, possibly elsewhere in the building, but perhaps in the even remoter porcelain of the Grebes, Mallards or Hoopoes, someone pulled a plug, and whoosh! It was lucky we hadn't been caught before, I told her. Only the merest chance had slotted us in the safety-spot between eruptions, and I would have gone on to counsel extreme alertness during the rest of our stay, only she was falling about helpless with laughter, the silly little creep. And do you, or do you not, find this typical of the sex? When a man's in no position to stand on his dignity, you can bet they'll come tramping right in and stand on it for him. Women have been left for less, it wouldn't surprise me. Anyway, I noticed she took good care not to risk it after that. Even left for the airport without –

'In Japan you have to go on the roof,' said Mrs A, yawning.

'Look at your knees,' said Mr A quickly.

'Where?' said Mrs A, sitting up with straight legs.

'Oh, never mind,' said Mr A. 'You've never been to Japan.'

'With everyone standing round watching, in very, very beautiful cherry-tree attitudes. It's a cemerony,' she said, drowsily.

'Ceremony.'

'I read somewhere. But they have them on the ground too, with those concrete footprints, like at New Corinth,' said Mrs A.

'And Sparta.'

'And Lassithi.'

'And Casablanca.'

'And Portofino.'

'And the place near Mount Parnassus,' said Mr A, 'where it was a hundred in the shade and we thought we were buying ice creams and they were those appalling sticky honeyburgers, and you made me go and put them down the – '

'Livadia, that was. They have the footprints at Boulogne.'

'I don't see how you can mention Parnassus and Boulogne in the same breath.'

'I don't see how you can mention breath in the same breath' said Mrs A. 'Talking of Parnassus, you don't know how near you were to death when you kept yelling Come and drink from the Castalian spring, and it was gushing and gurgling in mad abandon and all I wanted was a Ladies. They're smaller in Japan, I expect.'

'The ladies?'

'Those too. I was thinking of the concrete footprints.'

'Cause and effect,' said Mr A.

'Old Mrs Middleton won't go anywhere abroad except where they've had coastal batteries. She's written it in her phrase book in six languages, Please direct me without delay to an abandoned gun emplacement. She's got a dog called Martello.'

'Remember that godsend on the way to Ravenna? When we'd given up all hope, and then found that lonely demolished villa with its Grade A amenity in full working order, miraculously survived the bombing?'

'And when we were ready to call again on the way back – '

'All the men were on the job, demolishing.'

'And we realized,' said Mrs A, 'that we'd just struck lucky with their siesta the first time.'

'We had our bits of luck, certainly,' said Mr A. 'And on a lovely evening like this, with a nice pink sunset coming up through the beech hedge, and the court fast asleep with its notebook dropped, it doesn't do any harm to count our blessings. Like that WC sign turned the wrong way round at Hierapetra, and me just hurrying in when I see this Cretan grandma dishing up supper for eight.'

'Pachiammos was near Hierapetra,' said Mrs A. 'That was where a Cretan grandma wouldn't show me where it was until I'd eaten the plate of buns. I'm going to hate this session closing without giving my voluntary statement on that.'

'The Case of the Running Nun at La Rochelle shows you in a better light.'

'Does it?'

'Oh, yes. It was your apotheosis.'

'You're just saying that.'

'Not at all. We could have sustained lasting damage, sitting in the car in those rain-soaked docks, parked by a house that kept sloshing its bath overflow down our bit of gutter and not a glint of relief in sight. It was water, water everywhere, all right. I've said it before, and I'll say it again, if you hadn't spotted the Sister of Mercy belting over the cobbles with her skirts hitched up, and streaking round the back of the Clerk of the Works' hut – '

'Be fair to yourself, darling. We both spotted her.'

'You were the Perry Mason, darling. You drew the vital inference.'

'If you say so. But you were the one that had the terrible suspense at Pachiammos. How long was it you waited in the street after the policeman had taken me off to see his mother?'

'I always say three quarters of an hour, but it might only have been forty minutes. In any case, it must have been worse for you.'

'Ah,' said Mrs A, 'but at least I knew what was happening. She had to cook the buns first, so I could smell that . . . after she'd fetched a special chair for me from upstairs, and dusted it, and given me a glass of cold white wine and hung around so that I couldn't tip it into a vase. Then it was the buns. Then ten minutes conversation in sign language about her late husband's photograph and the olive crop. She said there were nine million olive trees on Crete, wrote it down, very slow and trembly, and I thought the next thing would be going out and counting them, before she finally led me to it and heaved the donkey from in front of the door.'

'I remember you looked radiant when you came back,' said Mr A.

'You didn't,' she said.

They sat for a time, thinking.

'I suppose we can hardly wake the court,' said Mrs A, beginning to collect cushions and glasses. 'But it's a pity he's missed so much.'

'He'd have suppressed it in any case,' said Mr A. He unstoppered the air bed, releasing its insignificant gust. 'For some reason, they always do.'

EPILOGUE

'RIGHT. Lights out,' said Mr A.

The screen filled with a dog, backing into a kennel upside down. 'I'm just using the old Spot sequence as a leader,' said Mr A. 'You'll find La Faute the right way up. Hello, something's stuck. Lights on, just a minute.'

Q. *This is your recent holiday we're going to see?*
A. *That's right. Has the court anything I can poke this sprocket with? Thank you.*
Q. *With the money troubles?*
A. *That's right.*
Q. *And the motor accident?*
A. *That's the one.*
Q. *When you missed the truffles?*
A. *I think one of these — yes, that's right — joins has parted.*
Q. *And you thought the police were after you? And had the terrible adventure in the Avenue of the Cormorants? And had to go to Poitiers when you didn't want to? And —*
A. *I'll be with you in a minute.*
Q. *— And got a Camembert cheese trapped in the window, and ran over your Thermos when you were nearly lynched in Malvenue-la-Bastide?*
A. *True. What about it?*
Q. *Only that with such a record of mishaps, what was there to make a movie of?*
A. *All set now. What? Oh, no, I think the court's got quite the wrong idea, I can't think why. Nothing more boring than being a sundial.*
Q. *I beg your — ?*
A. *Only telling the happy hours, you know, like the inscription says. We save those for the movie. We had a marvellous time, really, didn't we, darling? Always do. After all, the court's only been interested in the stresses and strains on the marriage, and we've tried to do our best for it. The sun and the fun, the long lazy hours away from it all on golden beaches — that's for the camera. Right. Lights out. Here we go. The jetty at La Faute. Two lovely days we had there. Nothing in it for the matrimonial investigator, of course, because, well, just look at that . . .*

The sea was very blue, calm and empty.

'Wait for it,' said Mr A. 'Nice little panning shot here, laughing French fishermen.'

'No!' cried Mrs A in the darkness.

The surface of the sea broke, and a pink bathing cap bobbed up, blowing seaweed.

'Here comes Mother Neptune,' said Mr A. 'The Monster of the Deep.'

'Swine,' said Mrs A.

But, in the court's view, the court is bound to say, there was hardly any malice in it.

INDEX

———